Everything's Coming Up Fractions
with Cuisenaire® Rods

by

John Bradford

NO LONGER THE PROPERTY
OF THE
UNIVERSITY OF R.I. LIBRARY

Cuisenaire Company of America, Inc.
12 Church Street
New Rochelle, NY 10801

Young

Copyright © 1981 by
Cuisenaire Company of America, Inc.
12 Church Street, New Rochelle, NY 10801

ISBN 0914040-91-X

The name Cuisenaire and the color sequence of the rods
are trademarks of the Cuisenaire Company of American, Inc.

Permission is granted for limited reproduction of pages from this book for classroom use.

Printed in U.S.A.

Introductory Notes

This beginning book on fractions is primarily intended for students in grades 4-6, but may be used wherever concrete models of fractions are needed to promote understanding and computational skill. No previous experience with Cuisenaire rods is assumed. Rod relationships and colors may be learned as students work on the meaning of fractions in the first few pages.

Meaning of fractions is emphasized throughout by constant reference to rod models. Initial work with equivalent fractions, inequalities, addition of fractions, and subtraction of fractions is all done with reference to a rod model and with no attempt to develop abstract procedures. The teacher should avoid any reference to abstract procedures in this initial stage. Students who find answers to addition problems by placing rods end-to-end and matching the result with a model should not fall into the common type of error illustrated by $1/2 + 1/3 = 2/5$. Only after much experience with concrete models is the abstract procedure for producing equivalent fractions and finding common denominators introduced. Even then, results often should be verified with a rod model. If students make errors, they should be asked to show their work with a rod model. After considerable experience with rods, many students will be able to add and substract fractions in their heads without pencil and paper.

Most fractions in this book are proper fractions (less than one). There is work with improper fractions or mixed numbers on page 41 only. The work with inequalities assumes a knowledge of the meaning of the symbols "$<$ and $>$". Fraction sentences are used in a manner which builds background for similar work with percent problems and algebraic equations. Riddles are used for their appeal to students and as a self-checking mechanism.

Complete answers are given on pages 50-59.

Please share your experiences, comments, and suggestions with us!

EVERYTHINGS COMING UP FRACTIONS
w/ Cuisenaire Rods

Table of Contents

Unit Fractions (Numerator is 1.)

Rod Color Names	1
Two Equal Pieces Show One-half ($\frac{1}{2}$)	2
One-Half or Not?	3
Riddle: Why Isn't Your Nose Twelve Inches Long?	4
One-Third or Not?	5
Thirds and Fourths or Not?	6
Riddle: How Many Hamburgers Can You Eat on an Empty Stomach?	7
Some Other Fractions	8
Riddle: What's the Difference between a Thief and a Church Bell?	9
One-Color Trains	10
Records of One-Color Trains with Fraction Sentences	11-12
One-Color Trains with Fraction Sentences	13-14
Completing Fraction Sentences	15
Filling in Missing Parts in Sentences with Rod Codes	16

Non-Unit Fractions (Numerator is not 1.)

Non-Unit Fractions	17-18
Riddle: What is the Principal Part of a Horse?	19
Riddle: What is the Difference between a Hill and a Pill	20

Equality and Inequality of Fractions

Ratios and Equivalent Fractions	21
Fractional Parts from Rod Trains	22-23
More Ratios and Equivalent Fractions	24
One-Color Trains and Equivalent Fractions	25-26
Comparing Fractional Parts	27
Riddle: What's More Earth-Shattering Than an Elephant Playing Hopscotch?	28
Riddle: What Do You Get If You Cross an Elephant and a Cactus?	29
Riddle: What Did Tillie Ask? What Did Millie Answer?	30
Families of One Color Trains and Lowest Terms	31-32

Addition of Fractions

Introducing Addition of Fractions with Rods 33

Adding Fractions with Rods 34-35

Riddle I: What Coat Is Put on Only When It's Wet?

    II: What Do You Say When You Call Your Dog and He
        Doesn't Come? 36

Riddle: What Happens to Two Frogs Who Try to Catch the Same Bug
    at the Same Time? 37

Riddle: What's the Difference Between a Man Going Up the Stairs
    and a Man Looking Up the Stairs? 38

Using Common Denominators to Add Fractions 39

Riddle: What Has One Horn, Runs Up and Down the Street,
    and Gives Milk? 40

Addition Problems with Sums Greater Than One 41

Subtraction of Fractions

Introducing Subtraction of Fractions with Rods 42

Subtracting Fractions Using Rods 43-44

Riddle: What's the Difference Between an Angry Rabbit and a
    Counterfeit $10 Bill? 45

Using Common Denominators to Subtract Fractions 46-47

Addition and Subtraction of Fractions

Riddle: What Has a Foot at Each End and a Foot in the Middle? 48

Riddle: What Happens to a Dog Who Eats Table Scraps? 49

Answers and Commentary 50-59

Rod Color Names

Cover the staircase with the rod that fits each space.

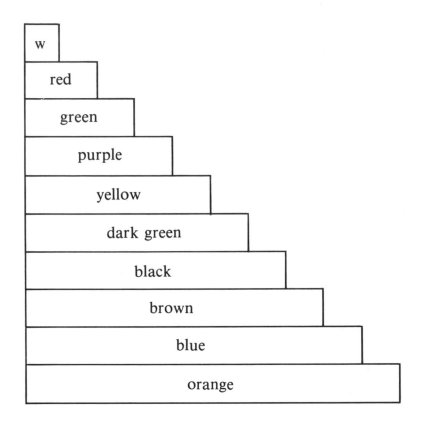

Predict the color of the rod which fits each drawing below.
Write the color name on each rod picture and check by covering with that colored rod.

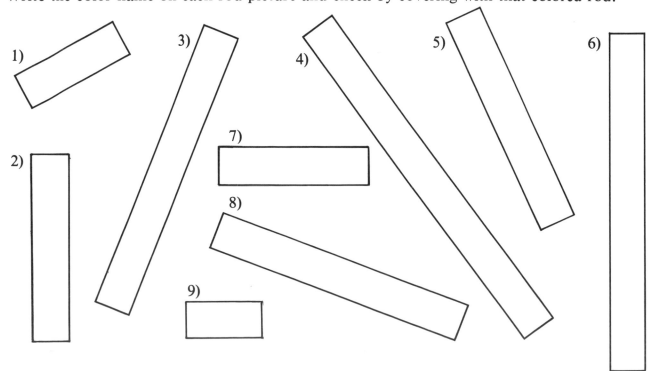

Everything's Coming up Fractions with Cuisenaire Rods   © 1981 Cuisenaire Company of America, Inc.

Two Equal Pieces Show One-Half ($\frac{1}{2}$)

Place your rods on each pattern to show $\frac{1}{2}$.

1)
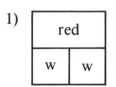

White is $\frac{1}{2}$ of red.

2)
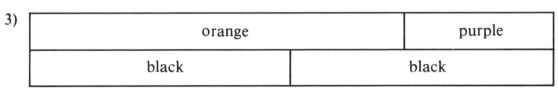

Purple is $\frac{1}{2}$ of brown.

3)
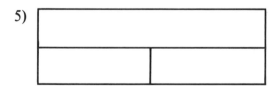

Black is $\frac{1}{2}$ of (orange & purple).

Place rods on each pattern below. Then draw an arrow to match each sentence with the correct pattern.

4)
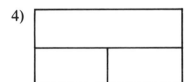

5)
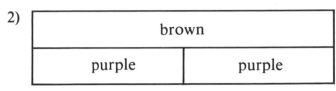

(A) Red is $\frac{1}{2}$ of purple.

(B) Dark green is $\frac{1}{2}$ of (orange & red).

(C) Green is $\frac{1}{2}$ of dark green.

6)
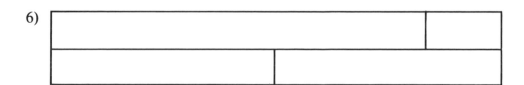

Everything's Coming up Fractions with Cuisenaire Rods   © 1981 Cuisenaire Company of America, Inc.

One-Half or Not?

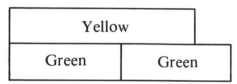

Green is *not* $\frac{1}{2}$ of yellow.

Place rods on each pattern below. Then draw an arrow to match each sentence with the correct pattern.

1)

2)

3)

A) Red is *not* $\frac{1}{2}$ of yellow.
B) Yellow is $\frac{1}{2}$ of orange.
C) Green is $\frac{1}{2}$ of dark green.
D) Black is *not* $\frac{1}{2}$ of (orange & green).
E) Purple is *not* $\frac{1}{2}$ of blue.

4)

5)

3

RIDDLE: Why Isn't Your Nose Twelve Inches Long?

The answer to this riddle is written in code at the bottom of the page. To break the code, use rods to work the problems below. If the statement is true, circle the letter in the column labeled true. If the statement is false, circle the letter in the column labeled false. Match the circled letters with the problem numbers to decode the answer to the riddle at the bottom of the page.

Prob.	True	False	Statement
1	T	R	Purple is $\frac{1}{2}$ of brown.
2	I	A	Yellow is $\frac{1}{2}$ of blue.
3	W	L	Red is $\frac{1}{2}$ of purple.
4	M	B	Green is $\frac{1}{2}$ of yellow.
5	S	N	Purple is $\frac{1}{2}$ of blue.
6	I	A	Yellow is $\frac{1}{2}$ of orange.
7	E	U	Green is $\frac{1}{2}$ of black.
8	F	P	Black is $\frac{1}{2}$ of (orange & purple).
9	T	D	Blue is $\frac{1}{2}$ of (orange & black).
10	L	W	Dark green is $\frac{1}{2}$ of (orange & red).
11	D	C	Brown is $\frac{1}{2}$ of (orange & black).
12	S	U	Blue is $\frac{1}{2}$ of (orange & brown).
13	N	H	Brown is $\frac{1}{2}$ of (orange & yellow).
14	B	O	Purple is $\frac{1}{2}$ of black.
15	E	I	Brown is $\frac{1}{2}$ of (orange & dark green).

Riddle Answer

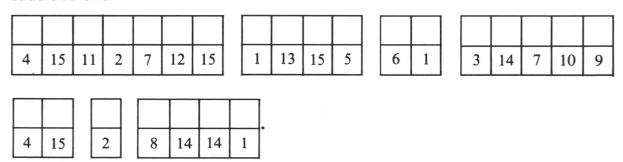

4	15	11	2	7	12	15		1	13	15	5		6	1		3	14	7	10	9

4	15		2		8	14	14	1

Everything's Coming up Fractions with Cuisenaire Rods   © 1981 Cuisenaire Company of America, Inc.

One-Third or Not?

Examples: (Place rods on the patterns.)

1) Since three white rods match a green rod, white is $\frac{1}{3}$ of green.

2) Since three green rods do not match an orange rod, green is *not* $\frac{1}{3}$ of orange.

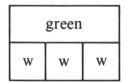

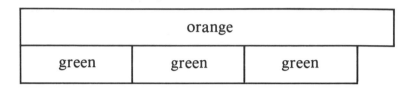

3) Since three purple rods match (orange & red), purple is $\frac{1}{3}$ of (orange & red).

orange		red
purple	purple	purple

Place rods on each pattern below. Then draw an arrow to match each sentence with the correct pattern.

4)

5)

6)

(A) Red is *not* $\frac{1}{3}$ of black.

(B) Green is $\frac{1}{3}$ of blue.

(C) White is *not* $\frac{1}{3}$ of purple.

(D) Red is $\frac{1}{3}$ of dark green.

7)

5

Thirds And Fourths Or Not?

Place rods on each pattern below. Then draw an arrow to match each sentence with the correct pattern.

1)

2)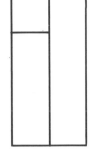

3)

(A) Green is *not* $\frac{1}{3}$ of orange.

(B) White is $\frac{1}{3}$ of green.

(C) Red is *not* $\frac{1}{3}$ of yellow.

(D) Green is $\frac{1}{3}$ of blue.

4)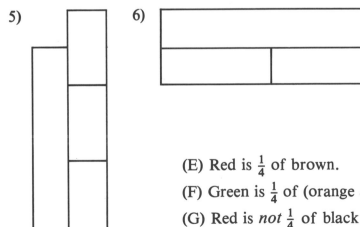

5)

6)

7)

(E) Red is $\frac{1}{4}$ of brown.

(F) Green is $\frac{1}{4}$ of (orange & red).

(G) Red is *not* $\frac{1}{4}$ of black.

(H) Green is *not* $\frac{1}{4}$ of (orange & green).

8)

Everything's Coming up Fractions with Cuisenaire Rods   © 1981 Cuisenaire Company of America, Inc.

RIDDLE: How Many Hamburgers Can You Eat On An Empty Stomach?

The answer to this riddle is written in code at the bottom of the page. To break this code, use rods to work the problems below. If the statement is true, circle the letter in the column labeled true. If the statement is false, circle the letter in the column labeled false. Match the circled letters with the problem numbers to answer the riddle at the bottom of the page.

Prob.	True	False	Statement
1	Y	R	Red is $\frac{1}{3}$ of dark green.
2	D	F	Green is $\frac{1}{3}$ of brown.
3	H	C	Yellow is $\frac{1}{3}$ of (orange & purple).
4	O	I	Purple is $\frac{1}{3}$ of (orange & red).
5	T	H	Dark green is $\frac{1}{3}$ of (orange & blue).
6	N	L	Black is $\frac{1}{3}$ of (orange & orange).
7	T	S	Yellow is $\frac{1}{3}$ of (orange & yellow).
8	M	X	Dark green is $\frac{1}{3}$ of (orange & brown).
9	P	B	White is $\frac{1}{4}$ of purple.
10	R	C	Purple is $\frac{1}{4}$ of (orange & dark green).
11	I	E	Yellow is $\frac{1}{4}$ of (orange & orange).
12	G	S	Black is $\frac{1}{4}$ of (orange & orange & blue).
13	U	J	Dark green is $\frac{1}{4}$ of (orange & orange & purple).
14	R	A	Brown is $\frac{1}{4}$ of (orange & orange & orange).
15	E	I	Black is $\frac{1}{4}$ of (orange & orange & brown).
16	N	Y	Brown is $\frac{1}{4}$ of (orange & orange & orange & red).

Riddle Answer

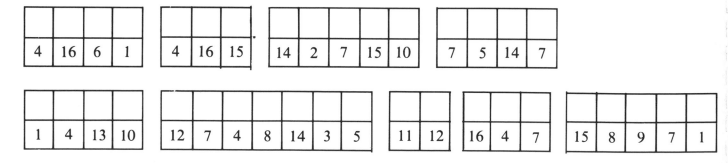

4	16	6	1

4	16	15

14	2	7	15	10

7	5	14	7

1	4	13	10

12	7	4	8	14	3	5

11	12

16	4	7

15	8	9	7	1

7

Everything's Coming up Fractions with Cuisenaire Rods © 1981 Cuisenaire Company of America, Inc.

Some Other Fractions

Place rods on each pattern below. Then draw an arrow to match each sentence with the correct pattern.

1)

3)

2)

(A) White is $\frac{1}{6}$ of dark green.

(B) Red is *not* $\frac{1}{5}$ of blue.

(C) White is *not* $\frac{1}{6}$ of black.

(D) Red is $\frac{1}{5}$ of orange.

4)

5)

6)

7)

(E) White is *not* $\frac{1}{8}$ of blue.

(F) Red is $\frac{1}{7}$ of (orange & purple).

(G) White is $\frac{1}{7}$ of black.

(H) Red is *not* $\frac{1}{7}$ of (orange & green).

8)

Everything's Coming up Fractions with Cuisenaire Rods   © 1981 Cuisenaire Company of America, Inc.

Riddle: What's The Difference Between A Thief And A Church Bell?

The answer to this riddle is written in code at the bottom of the page. To break this code, use rods to work the problems below. If the statement is true, circle the letter in the column labeled true. If the statement is false, circle the letter in the column labeled false. Match the circled letters with the problem numbers to answer the riddle at the bottom of the page.

Prob.	True	False	Statement
1	S	B	White is $\frac{1}{10}$ of orange.
2	L	V	White is $\frac{1}{7}$ of black.
3	O	E	Green is $\frac{1}{6}$ of (orange & brown).
4	T	M	Red is $\frac{1}{7}$ of (orange & yellow).
5	S	E	Red is $\frac{1}{6}$ of (orange & green).
6	W	R	Red is $\frac{1}{9}$ of (orange & blue).
7	Y	T	Purple is $\frac{1}{6}$ of (orange & orange & yellow).
8	F	A	Red is $\frac{1}{8}$ of (orange & dark green).
9	N	U	Green is $\frac{1}{5}$ of (orange & yellow).
10	C	P	Yellow is $\frac{1}{5}$ of (orange & orange & purple).
11	H	D	Purple is $\frac{1}{5}$ of (orange & orange).
12	Y	A	Green is $\frac{1}{7}$ of (orange & orange & red).

Riddle Answer

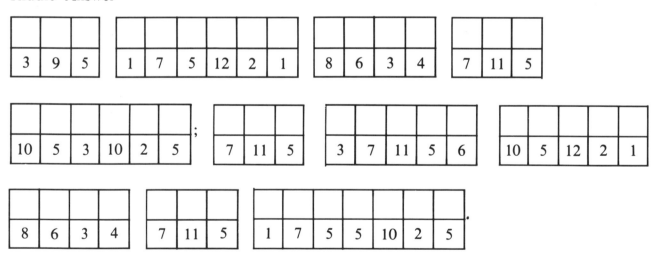

Everything's Coming up Fractions with Cuisenaire Rods   © 1981 Cuisenaire Company of America, Inc.

One-Color Trains

Make all the one-color trains for each rod. Put the number of rods of each color in the ◯.

Example:

dark green		
green		green
red	red	red
w	w	w	w	w	w

One-color trains

a) (2) green _____

b) (3) red _____

c) (6) white _____

Complete each of the following:

1)

blue

a) ◯ green _____

b) ◯ white _____

2)

brown
Build one-color trains here

a) ◯ purple _____

b) ◯ red _____

c) ◯ white _____

3)

orange
Build one-color trains here

a) ◯ yellow _____

b) ◯ red _____

c) ◯ white _____

Everything's Coming up Fractions with Cuisenaire Rods   © 1981 Cuisenaire Company of America, Inc.

Records Of One-Color Trains With Fraction Sentences

Make all the one-color trains for each rod. Complete the records by filling in the blanks showing the color of each train, the number of rods needed to make it, and the fraction sentence suggested by that train.

Example:

brown							
purple				purple			
red		red		red		red	
w	w	w	w	w	w	w	w

Record

Color of train	Number of rods	Fraction sentence
a) purple	2	$\frac{1}{2}$ of brown = purple.
b) red	4	$\frac{1}{4}$ of brown = red.
c) white	8	$\frac{1}{8}$ of brown = white.

1)

purple	
red	red
w	w	w	w

Record

Color of train	Number of rods	Fraction sentence
a) red		$\frac{1}{2}$ of purple = _____ .
b)	4	$\frac{1}{4}$ of purple = _____ .

2)

black						
w	w	w	w	w	w	w

Record

Color of train	Number of rods	Fraction sentence
a) white		$\frac{1}{7}$ of black = _____ .

3)

dark green		
green		green
red	red	red
w	w	w	w	w	w

Record

Color of train	Number of rods	Fraction sentence
a) green		$\frac{1}{2}$ of dark green = _____ .
b)	3	$\frac{1}{3}$ of dark green = _____ .
c) white		$\frac{1}{6}$ of dark green = _____ .

11

More Records Of One-Color Trains with Fraction Sentences

Make all the one-color trains for each rod or rod combination. Complete the record by listing the color of each train, the number of rods needed to make it, and the fraction sentence suggested by that train.

Example:

blue
green	green	green
w	w	w	w	w	w	w	w	w

Record

Color of train	Number of rods	Fraction sentence
a) green	3	$\boxed{\frac{1}{3}}$ of blue = green.
b) white	9	$\boxed{\frac{1}{9}}$ of blue = white.

1)

orange
yellow	yellow
red	red	red	red	red
w	w	w	w	w	w	w	w	w	w

Record

Color of train	Number of rods	Fraction sentence
a)		⬡ of orange = _____
b)		⬡ of orange = _____
c)		⬡ of orange = _____

2)

orange	red

Build one-color trains here.

Record

Color of train	Number of rods	Fraction sentence
a)		⬡ of (orange & red) = _____
b)		⬡ of (orange & red) = _____
c)		⬡ of (orange & red) = _____
d)		⬡ of (orange & red) = _____
e)		⬡ of (orange & red) = _____

Everything's Coming up Fractions with Cuisenaire Rods   © 1981 Cuisenaire Company of America, Inc.

One-Color Trains With Fraction Sentences

Make all the one-color trains for each rod combination and then complete each fraction sentence.

1)

orange	purple

Build one-color trains here.

Fraction sentence

⬡ of (orange & purple) = _____ .

⬡ of (orange & purple) = _____ .

⬡ of (orange & purple) = _____ .

2)

orange	yellow

Build one-color trains here.

Fraction sentence

⬡ of (orange & yellow) = _____ .

⬡ of (orange & yellow) = _____ .

⬡ of (orange & yellow) = _____ .

3)

orange	dark green

Build one-color trains here.

Fraction sentence

⬡ of (orange & dark green) = _____ .

⬡ of (orange & dark green) = _____ .

⬡ of (orange & dark green) = _____ .

⬡ of (orange & dark green) = _____ .

13

More One-Color Trains With Fraction Sentences

Make all the one-color trains for each rod combination and then complete each fraction sentence.

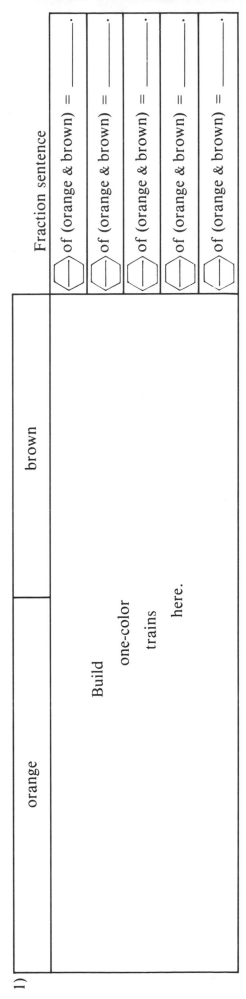

1)

orange	brown
	Build one-color trains here.

Fraction sentence

◯— of (orange & brown) = ⋯
◯— of (orange & brown) = ⋯
◯— of (orange & brown) = ⋯
◯— of (orange & brown) = ⋯
◯— of (orange & brown) = ⋯

On your desk make all the one-color trains for each rod combination named below and then complete each fraction sentence.

2) orange & orange
Fraction sentences.

⬡$\frac{1}{2}$ of (orange & orange) = ⋯
⬡$\frac{1}{4}$ of (orange & orange) = ⋯
⬡$\frac{1}{5}$ of (orange & orange) = ⋯
⬡$\frac{1}{10}$ of (orange & orange) = ⋯
⬡$\frac{1}{20}$ of (orange & orange) = ⋯

3) orange & orange & white
Fraction sentences

◯— of (orange & orange & white) = ⋯
◯— of (orange & orange & white) = ⋯
◯— of (orange & orange & white) = ⋯

14

Everything's Coming up Fractions with Cuisenaire Rods © 1981 Cuisenaire Company of America, Inc.

Completing Fraction Sentences

Fill in the color name for the rod which makes each sentence true. Use your rods to find the solutions.

Example I:
Green is $\frac{1}{3}$ of _____ .

Solution:
Line up *three* green rods.

blue		
green	green	green

Since *three* green rods match blue, green is $\frac{1}{3}$ of *blue*.

Example II:

_____ is $\frac{1}{4}$ of (orange & dark green).

Solution:
Line up (orange & dark green) and match with *four* rods of the same color.

orange		dark green	
purple	purple	purple	purple

Since *four* purple rods match (orange & dark green), *purple* is $\frac{1}{4}$ of (orange & dark green).

Problems:

1) _____ is $\frac{1}{4}$ of brown.

2) _____ is $\frac{1}{3}$ of green.

3) Purple is $\frac{1}{3}$ of (orange & _____).

4) _____ is $\frac{1}{5}$ of orange.

5) Green is $\frac{1}{6}$ of (orange & _____).

6) _____ is $\frac{1}{2}$ of (orange & dark green).

7) Dark green is $\frac{1}{3}$ of (orange & _____).

8) White is $\frac{1}{7}$ of _____ .

9) _____ is $\frac{1}{3}$ of (orange & orange & white).

10) Red is $\frac{1}{6}$ of (orange & _____).

11) _____ is $\frac{1}{5}$ of (orange & yellow).

12) White is $\frac{1}{9}$ of _____ .

Everything's Coming up Fractions with Cuisenaire Rods   © 1981 Cuisenaire Company of America, Inc.

Filling In Missing Parts In Sentences With Rod Codes

Rod Codes

White	Red	Green	Purple	Yellow	Dark green	blacK	browN	bluE	Orange
W	R	G	P	Y	D	K	N	E	O

First letters   Last letters   First letter

Use your rods to find the rod color which makes each sentence true. Use the chart above to write your answers in rod code. Then check the answers by filling in the crossword puzzle below with the rod code letter you found for each problem. (Problem 1 has been done for you.)

Think: The answer is white. The code is W.

1) $\frac{1}{8}$ of brown = $\boxed{W}$.

2) $\frac{1}{4}$ of (orange & dark green) = $\boxed{}$.

3) $\frac{1}{8}$ of (orange & dark green) = $\boxed{}$.

4) $\frac{1}{5}$ of $\boxed{}$ = red.

5) $\frac{1}{3}$ of $\boxed{}$ = red.

6) $\frac{1}{10}$ of $\boxed{}$ = white.

7) $\frac{1}{3}$ of $\boxed{}$ = green.

8) $\frac{1}{13}$ of (orange & green) = $\boxed{}$.

9) $\frac{1}{7}$ of (orange & purple) = $\boxed{}$.

10) $\frac{1}{5}$ of (orange & orange) = $\boxed{}$.

11) $\frac{1}{9}$ of $\boxed{}$ = white.

12) $\frac{1}{2}$ of (orange & brown) = $\boxed{}$.

13) $\frac{1}{2}$ of (orange & purple) = $\boxed{}$.

14) $\frac{1}{3}$ of (orange & brown) = $\boxed{}$.

15) $\frac{1}{9}$ of (orange & brown) = $\boxed{}$.

16) $\frac{1}{2}$ of (orange & orange) = $\boxed{}$.

17) $\frac{1}{6}$ of (orange & orange & purple) = $\boxed{}$.

18) $\frac{1}{4}$ of (orange & orange & purple) = $\boxed{}$.

19) $\frac{1}{3}$ of (orange & yellow) = $\boxed{}$.

20) $\frac{1}{3}$ of (orange & orange & black) = $\boxed{}$.

21) $\frac{1}{8}$ of (orange & orange & purple) = $\boxed{}$.

22) $\frac{1}{10}$ of (orange & orange) = $\boxed{}$.

23) $\frac{1}{3}$ of (orange & orange & orange) = $\boxed{}$.

24) $\frac{1}{6}$ of (dark green) = $\boxed{}$.

Crossword Answers

16

Everything's Coming up Fractions with Cuisenaire Rods   © 1981 Cuisenaire Company of America, Inc.

Non-Unit Fractions

The shaded parts of the drawings below show non-unit fractions of several rods. A non-unit fraction is one like $\frac{2}{3}$, $\frac{3}{4}$, $\frac{7}{10}$, etc. where the top number (numerator) is not 1.

Example I:

   If $\frac{1}{3}$ of green = 1 white

   $\frac{2}{3}$ of green = 2 whites

green		
w	w	w

Example II:

   If $\frac{1}{4}$ of brown = 1 red

   $\frac{3}{4}$ of brown = 3 reds.

brown			
red	red	red	red

Complete the sentence by filling in the rod color name for the non-unit fraction shaded in each diagram.

1) If $\frac{1}{3}$ of dark green = 1 red

   $\frac{2}{3}$ of dark green = _____ .

dark green		
red	red	red

2) If $\frac{1}{5}$ of orange = 1 red

   $\frac{3}{5}$ of orange = _____ .

orange				
red	red	red	red	red

3) If $\frac{1}{8}$ of brown = 1 white.

   $\frac{3}{8}$ of brown = _____ .

brown							
w	w	w	w	w	w	w	w

17

Everything's Coming up Fractions with Cuisenaire Rods © 1981 Cuisenaire Company of America, Inc.

Non-Unit Fractions

Complete the sentence by filling in the rod color name for the non-unit fraction shaded in each diagram.

1) If $\frac{1}{3}$ of blue = green

   $\frac{2}{3}$ of blue = _____.

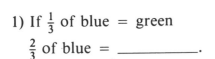

2) If $\frac{1}{8}$ of brown = white

   $\frac{5}{8}$ of brown = _____.

3) If $\frac{1}{4}$ of purple = white

   $\frac{3}{4}$ of purple = _____.

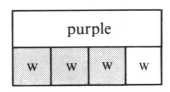

4) If $\frac{1}{7}$ of black = white

   $\frac{6}{7}$ of black = _____.

5) If $\frac{1}{3}$ of (orange & red) = purple

   $\frac{2}{3}$ of (orange & red) = _____.

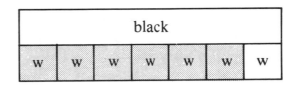

6) If $\frac{1}{4}$ of (orange & red) = green

   $\frac{3}{4}$ of (orange & red) = _____.

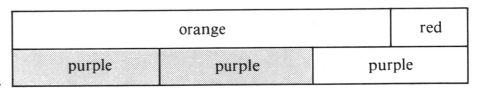

18

Everything's Coming up Fractions with Cuisenaire Rods   © 1981 Cuisenaire Company of America, Inc.

RIDDLE: What Is The Principal Part of a Horse?

The answer to this riddle is written in code at the bottom of the page. To solve the riddle, work each problem below by filling in the ⬡ with the fraction represented by the rods in the shaded part of the drawing. For problems 1 - 5 use Table I to match the fraction answer with a problem number and a letter. For problems 6 - 8 use Table II.

1) Dark green = ⬡ of (orange & red).

2) Two purples = ⬡ of (orange & red).

3) Three greens = ⬡ of (orange & red).

4) Five reds = ⬡ of (orange & red).

5) Seven whites = ⬡ of (orange & red).

6) Black = ⬡ of (orange & purple).

7) Three reds = ⬡ of (orange & purple).

8) Five whites = ⬡ of (orange & purple).

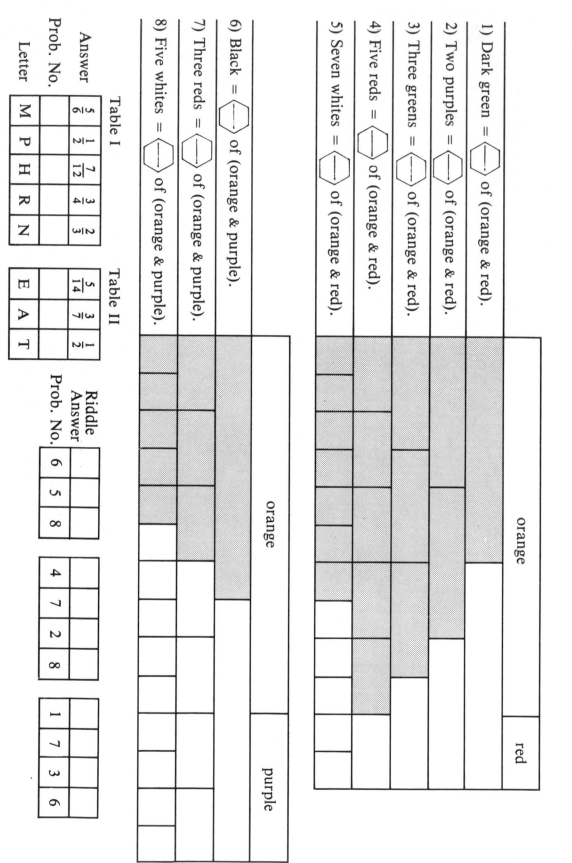

Table I

Answer	$\frac{5}{6}$	$\frac{1}{2}$	$\frac{7}{12}$	$\frac{3}{4}$	$\frac{2}{3}$
Prob. No.					
Letter	M	P	H	R	N

Table II

	$\frac{5}{14}$	$\frac{3}{7}$	$\frac{1}{2}$
	E	A	T

Prob. No.	6	5	8		4	7	2	8		1	7	3	6
Riddle Answer													

Everything's Coming up Fractions with Cuisenaire Rods   © 1981 Cuisenaire Company of America, Inc.

RIDDLE: What Is The Difference Between A Hill And A Pill?

The answer to this riddle is written in code at the bottom of the page. To break the code, work the problems below. For problems 1 - 8, use Table I to match the problem number with the rod code for the color name of the rod that makes the sentence true. For problems 9 - 16, use Table II to match the fraction answer with a problem number and letter.

Think: The answer is green. The code is G.

1) $\frac{2}{3}$ of blue = two ☐ G

2) $\frac{5}{8}$ of brown = five ☐

3) $\frac{4}{5}$ of orange = four ☐

4) $\frac{1}{2}$ of (orange & brown) = ☐

5) $\frac{2}{3}$ of three orange rods = two ☐

6) $\frac{2}{3}$ of orange & red = two ☐

7) $\frac{3}{4}$ of two orange & purple = three ☐

8) $\frac{4}{5}$ of four orange rods = four ☐

Fill in the missing fraction.

9) Three whites = ⬡ of black.

10) Five greens = ⬡ of orange & brown.

11) Seven reds = ⬡ of orange & dark green.

12) Two whites = ⬡ of blue.

13) Two whites = ⬡ of black.

14) Two blacks = ⬡ of two orange & white.

15) Nine whites = ⬡ of orange.

16) Three dark greens = ⬡ of two orange & purple.

Table I

	White	Red	Green	Purple	Yellow	Dark green	blacK	browN	bluE	Orange
Rod Codes:	W	R	G	P	Y	D	K	N	E	O

Table II

Answer	$\frac{3}{7}$	$\frac{3}{4}$	$\frac{2}{9}$	$\frac{9}{10}$	$\frac{2}{3}$	$\frac{2}{7}$	$\frac{7}{8}$	$\frac{5}{6}$
Prob. No.								
Letter	A	P	I	T	S	L	H	U

Riddle Answer

| 9 | | 11 | 12 | 13 | 13 | | 12 | 14 | | 11 | 9 | 3 | 7 | | 15 | 5 | | 1 | 4 | 15 | | 10 | 16 | . |

| 9 | | 6 | 12 | 13 | 13 | | 12 | 14 | | 11 | 9 | 3 | 7 | | 15 | 5 | | 1 | 4 | 15 | | 7 | 5 | 2 | 8 |

20

Everything's Coming up Fractions with Cuisenaire Rods   © 1981 Cuisenaire Company of America, Inc.

Ratios And Equivalent Fractions

Make all the one-color trains for the brown rod by covering the diagram below.

brown							
purple				purple			
red		red		red		red	
w	w	w	w	w	w	w	w

Example I:

Put a purple rod on top of your rod pattern. Move it up and down and see what it matches exactly. You should see that purple matches purple, two reds, and four whites. Purple is $\frac{1}{2}$ of brown. Since red is $\frac{1}{4}$ of brown, two reds are $\frac{2}{4}$ of brown. Since white is $\frac{1}{8}$ of brown, four whites are $\frac{4}{8}$ of brown. So, the purple rod matches $\frac{1}{2}$, $\frac{2}{4}$, and $\frac{4}{8}$ of brown. These fractional parts are equivalent, so we write: $\frac{purple}{brown} = \frac{1}{2} = \frac{2}{4} = \frac{4}{8}$.

Example II:

Put a dark green rod on top of your rod pattern. Move it up and down. It matches three reds ($\frac{3}{4}$) and six whites ($\frac{6}{8}$). So $\frac{dark\ green}{brown} = \frac{3}{4} = \frac{6}{8}$.

Example III:

Put a green rod on top of your rod pattern. Move it up and down. It matches three whites ($\frac{3}{8}$). So, $\frac{green}{brown} = \frac{3}{8}$. Also, $\frac{yellow}{brown} = \frac{5}{8}$ and $\frac{black}{brown} = \frac{7}{8}$.

Make all the one-color trains for dark green and complete the problems below.

dark green					
green			green		
red		red		red	
w	w	w	w	w	w

1) $\dfrac{green}{dark\ green} = \dfrac{1}{\boxed{2}} = \dfrac{3}{\square}$

2) $\dfrac{red}{dark\ green} = \dfrac{1}{\square} = \dfrac{\square}{6}$

3) $\dfrac{purple}{dark\ green} = \dfrac{\square}{3} = \dfrac{\square}{6}$

4) $\dfrac{yellow}{dark\ green} = \dfrac{\square}{6}$

21

Everything's Coming up Fractions with Cuisenaire Rods   © 1981 Cuisenaire Company of America, Inc.

Fractional Parts From Rod Trains

Place a purple rod between the heavy lines on the diagrams below and move it down the page. Stop wherever it matches up exactly with the rods in a train and complete the fraction sentence for that row by filling in the ⬡ .

Example:

dark green	
green	green
red	red	red
w	w	w	w	w	w

Purple is ⟨$\frac{2}{3}$⟩ of dark green.

Purple is ⟨$\frac{4}{6}$⟩ of dark green.

Problems:

1)

black	
w	w	w	w	w	w	w

Purple is ⟨——⟩ of black.

2)

orange	
yellow	yellow
red	red	red	red	red
w	w	w	w	w	w	w	w	w	w

Purple is ⟨——⟩ of orange.

Purple is ⟨——⟩ of orange.

3)

orange		red
dark green	dark green	
purple	purple	purple
green	green	green	green
red	red	red	red	red	red
w	w	w	w	w	w	w	w	w	w	w	w

Purple is ⟨——⟩ of (orange & red)

Purple is ⟨——⟩ of (orange & red)

Purple is ⟨——⟩ of (orange & red)

Everything's Coming up Fractions with Cuisenaire Rods   © 1981 Cuisenaire Company of America, Inc.

More Fractional Parts From Rod Trains

Place a dark green rod between the heavy lines on the diagrams below and move it down the page. Stop wherever it matches up exactly with the rods in a train and complete the fraction sentence for that row by filling in the (__ / __).

1)

brown			
purple		purple	
red	red	red	red
w	w	w	w	w	w	w	w

Dark green is (__ / __) of brown.

Dark green is (__ / __) of brown.

2)

blue		
green	green	green
w	w	w	w	w	w	w	w	w

Dark green is (__ / __) of blue.

Dark green is (__ / __) of blue.

3)

black	
w	w	w	w	w	w	w

Dark green is (__ / __) of black.

4)

orange		red	red	red
black			purple	
w	w	w	w	w	w	w	w	w	w

black			red	red	red	red
w	w	w	w	w	w	w	w	w	w	w	w	w	w

Dark green is (__ / __) of (orange & purple).

Dark green is (__ / __) of (orange & purple).

Dark green is (__ / __) of (orange & purple).

23

Everything's Coming up Fractions with Cuisenaire Rods   © 1981 Cuisenaire Company of America, Inc.

More Ratios And Equivalent Fractions

Make all the one-color trains for (orange & red) and complete the problems below.

orange									red	
dark green					dark green					
purple		purple		purple						
green		green		green		green				
red	red	red	red	red		red				
w	w	w	w	w	w	w	w	w	w	w	w

Example: $\dfrac{\text{dark green}}{\text{(orange \& red)}}$ = —— = —— = —— = ——

Put a dark green rod on top of your rod pattern. It matches dark green ($\frac{1}{2}$), two greens ($\frac{2}{4}$), three reds ($\frac{3}{6}$), and six whites ($\frac{6}{12}$).

So, $\dfrac{\text{dark green}}{\text{(orange \& red)}} = \frac{1}{2} = \frac{2}{4} = \frac{3}{6} = \frac{6}{12}$.

Problems:

1) $\dfrac{\text{purple}}{\text{(orange \& red)}}$ = —— = —— = ——

2) $\dfrac{\text{green}}{\text{(orange \& red)}}$ = —— = ——

3) $\dfrac{\text{red}}{\text{(orange \& red)}}$ = —— = ——

4) $\dfrac{\text{white}}{\text{(orange \& red)}}$ = ——

5) $\dfrac{\text{yellow}}{\text{(orange \& red)}}$ = ——

6) $\dfrac{\text{black}}{\text{(orange \& red)}}$ = ——

7) $\dfrac{\text{brown}}{\text{(orange \& red)}}$ = —— = —— = ——

8) $\dfrac{\text{blue}}{\text{(orange \& red)}}$ = —— = ——

9) $\dfrac{\text{orange}}{\text{(orange \& red)}}$ = —— = ——

10) $\dfrac{\text{(orange \& white)}}{\text{(orange \& red)}}$ = ——

24

One-Color Trains And Equivalent Fractions

Make all the one-color trains for an orange rod and complete the problems.

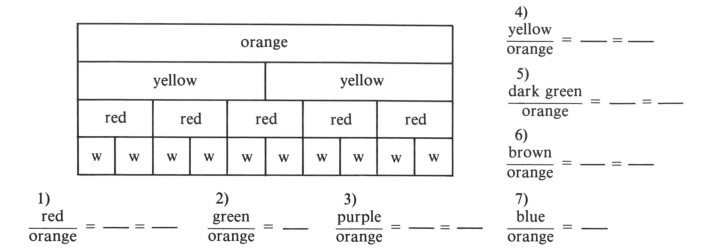

4)
$$\frac{\text{yellow}}{\text{orange}} = \underline{\quad} = \underline{\quad}$$

5)
$$\frac{\text{dark green}}{\text{orange}} = \underline{\quad} = \underline{\quad}$$

6)
$$\frac{\text{brown}}{\text{orange}} = \underline{\quad} = \underline{\quad}$$

1)
$$\frac{\text{red}}{\text{orange}} = \underline{\quad} = \underline{\quad}$$

2)
$$\frac{\text{green}}{\text{orange}} = \underline{\quad}$$

3)
$$\frac{\text{purple}}{\text{orange}} = \underline{\quad} = \underline{\quad}$$

7)
$$\frac{\text{blue}}{\text{orange}} = \underline{\quad}$$

Make all the one-color trains for (orange & brown) and complete the problems below.

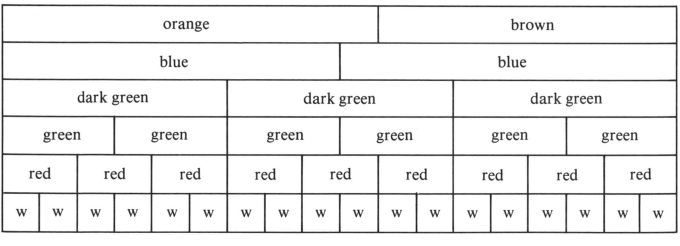

8)
$$\frac{\text{red}}{\text{(orange \& brown)}} = \underline{\quad} = \underline{\quad}$$

9)
$$\frac{\text{green}}{\text{(orange \& brown)}} = \underline{\quad} = \underline{\quad}$$

10)
$$\frac{\text{purple}}{\text{(orange \& brown)}} = \underline{\quad} = \underline{\quad}$$

11)
$$\frac{\text{yellow}}{\text{(orange \& brown)}} = \underline{\quad}$$

12)
$$\frac{\text{dark green}}{\text{(orange \& brown)}} = \underline{\quad} = \underline{\quad} = \underline{\quad} = \underline{\quad}$$

13)
$$\frac{\text{blue}}{\text{(orange \& brown)}} = \underline{\quad} = \underline{\quad} = \underline{\quad}$$

14)
$$\frac{\text{orange}}{\text{(orange \& brown)}} = \underline{\quad} = \underline{\quad}$$

15)
$$\frac{\text{(orange \& red)}}{\text{(orange \& brown)}} = \underline{\quad} = \underline{\quad} = \underline{\quad} = \underline{\quad}$$

16)
$$\frac{\text{(orange \& purple)}}{\text{(orange \& brown)}} = \underline{\quad} = \underline{\quad}$$

25

Everything's Coming up Fractions with Cuisenaire Rods   © 1981 Cuisenaire Company of America, Inc.

More One-Color Trains And Equivalent Fractions

Cover the diagram below to show the fractional parts for (orange & orange & purple).

Complete the problems below:

1) $\dfrac{\text{(orange \& red)}}{\text{(orange \& orange \& purple)}} = \dfrac{1}{2} = \dfrac{2}{4} = \dfrac{3}{6} = \underline{\quad} = \underline{\quad} = \dfrac{\quad}{24}$

2) $\dfrac{\text{brown}}{\text{(orange \& orange \& purple)}} = \dfrac{1}{3} = \underline{\quad} = \underline{\quad} = \underline{\quad}$

3) $\dfrac{\text{dark green}}{\text{(orange \& orange \& purple)}} = \underline{\quad} = \underline{\quad} = \underline{\quad}$

4) $\dfrac{\text{purple}}{\text{(orange \& orange \& purple)}} = \underline{\quad} = \underline{\quad} = \underline{\quad}$

5) $\dfrac{\text{(orange \& brown)}}{\text{(orange \& orange \& purple)}} = \dfrac{3}{4} = \dfrac{\quad}{8} = \underline{\quad} = \underline{\quad}$

6) $\dfrac{\text{red}}{\text{(orange \& orange \& purple)}} = \underline{\quad} = \underline{\quad}$

7) $\dfrac{\text{yellow}}{\text{(orange \& orange \& purple)}} = \underline{\quad} = \underline{\quad}$

8) $\dfrac{\text{green}}{\text{(orange \& orange \& purple)}} = \underline{\quad} = \underline{\quad}$

9) $\dfrac{\text{(orange \& purple)}}{\text{(orange \& orange \& purple)}} = \underline{\quad} = \underline{\quad}$

10) $\dfrac{\text{(orange \& yellow)}}{\text{(orange \& orange \& purple)}} = \underline{\quad} = \underline{\quad}$

26

Everything's Coming up Fractions with Cuisenaire Rods   © 1981 Cuisenaire Company of America, Inc.

RIDDLE: What Do You Get If You Cross An Elephant And A Cactus?

The answer to this riddle is written in code at the bottom of the page. For problems 1 - 6, use Table I to match the problem number with the rod code for the color name of the rod that makes the sentence true.

Cover the diagram with rods.

blue								
green			green			green		
w	w	w	w	w	w	w	w	w

1) $\frac{1}{3}$ of blue = ☐

2) $\frac{1}{9}$ of blue = ☐

3) $\frac{2}{9}$ of blue = ☐

4) $\frac{4}{9}$ of blue = ☐

5) $\frac{2}{3}$ of blue = ☐

6) $\frac{8}{9}$ of blue = ☐

Table I

	White	Red	Green	Purple	Yellow	Dark green	blacK	browN	bluE	Orange
Rod Codes:	W	R	G	P	Y	D	K	N	E	O

For problems 7 - 16, find the rods which are the given fractional parts of blue. Compare these to tell whether the statement in Table II is true or false. Circle the first letter for true, second for false. Then match the problem number with the circled letter.

Table II

Prob	True	False	Statement
7	R	T	$\frac{1}{3} < \frac{2}{9}$
8	A	E	$\frac{1}{9} > \frac{1}{3}$
9	I	L	$\frac{2}{9} < \frac{1}{3}$
10	M	U	$\frac{5}{9} = \frac{1}{3}$
11	O	Y	$\frac{6}{9} = \frac{2}{3}$

Prob	True	False	Statement
12	D	C	$\frac{8}{9} < \frac{2}{3}$
13	B	F	$\frac{2}{3} > \frac{5}{9}$
14	L	G	$\frac{1}{3} = \frac{3}{9}$
15	H	N	$\frac{2}{3} < \frac{7}{9}$
16	T	S	$\frac{1}{3} > \frac{4}{9}$

Riddle Answer

7	15	8

13	9	1	1	8	16	7

4	11	3	12	10	4	9	6	8

9	6

7	15	8

2	11	3	14	5

Everything's Coming up Fractions with Cuisenaire Rods   © 1981 Cuisenaire Company of America, Inc.

RIDDLE: What Did Tillie Ask? What Did Millie Answer?

The answers are written in code at the bottom of the page. For problems 1 - 10, use Table I to match the problem number with the rod code for the color name of the rod that makes the sentence true.

Problems 1 - 10: Before starting these problems, make all the one-color trains for the orange rod.

1) $\frac{1}{2}$ of orange = ☐   5) $\frac{3}{5}$ of orange = ☐   9) $\frac{4}{5}$ of orange = ☐

2) $\frac{1}{5}$ of orange = ☐   6) $\frac{3}{10}$ of orange = ☐   10) $\frac{9}{10}$ of orange = ☐

3) $\frac{1}{10}$ of orange = ☐   7) $\frac{4}{10}$ of orange = ☐

4) $\frac{2}{5}$ of orange = ☐   8) $\frac{7}{10}$ of orange = ☐

Table I

	White	Red	Green	Purple	Yellow	Dark green	blacK	browN	bluE	Orange
Rod Codes:	W	R	G	P	Y	D	K	N	E	O

For problems 11 - 20, find the rods which are the given fractional parts of orange. Compare the two rods to tell whether the statement in Table II is true or false. Circle the first letter for true, second for false. Then match the problem number with the circled letter.

Table II

Prob	True	False	Statement
11	M	D	$\frac{1}{5} > \frac{1}{2}$
12	A	I	$\frac{3}{10} > \frac{2}{5}$
13	O	U	$\frac{1}{2} < \frac{3}{5}$
14	V	W	$\frac{4}{10} = \frac{2}{5}$
15	L	P	$\frac{7}{10} > \frac{4}{5}$

Prob	True	False	Statement
16	L	Y	$\frac{8}{10} = \frac{4}{5}$
17	A	U	$\frac{5}{10} > \frac{3}{5}$
18	E	O	$\frac{2}{5} < \frac{1}{2}$
19	T	R	$\frac{6}{10} = \frac{3}{5}$
20	S	K	$\frac{1}{10} > \frac{1}{2}$

Tillie's Question

| 5 | 13 | | 1 | 13 | 17 | | 16 | 12 | 8 | 10 | | 8 | 12 | 4 | 16 | 12 | 9 | 6 | ?

Millie's Answer

| 12 | | 5 | 13 | 9 | 19 ' | | 8 | 9 | 13 | 3 | | 12 | 14 | 10 ' | . | 9 | 10 | 14 | 10 | 2 |

| 20 | 12 | 15 | 7 | 16 | 18 | 11 | .

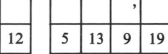

Everything's Coming up Fractions with Cuisenaire Rods   © 1981 Cuisenaire Company of America, Inc.

Families Of One-Color Trains And Lowest Terms

Just as you, your parents, and your brothers and sisters have a family name, we can think of the number of white rods which it takes to match a particular rod color as providing a family name. The one-color trains which match the particular color may have other names also, but they can always be described using the family name.

Example: Take a brown rod. Place white rods above the brown rod to emphasize the family name. Then make the other one-color trains, as shown in the diagram below.

w	w	w	w	w	w	w	w	←Family name (eighths)
brown								
purple				purple				
red		red		red		red		

Complete the table below. First place each color on the family name row above to determine the fraction using the family name. Then compare each color with the other one-color trains to find other possible names for the same fraction. Note that the other names use smaller numbers. When a fraction is expressed with the smallest possible numbers, it is in LOWEST TERMS. Circle the lowest terms for each problem.

	Rod color	Family name	Other names	
		Brown Rod Family (eighths)		
Examples →	purple	$\frac{4}{8}$	$\boxed{\frac{1}{2}}$, $\frac{2}{4}$	$\frac{1}{2}$ is in lowest terms
	green	$\boxed{\frac{3}{8}}$	none	$\frac{3}{8}$ is in lowest terms
	red	$\frac{2}{8}$	$\boxed{\frac{1}{4}}$	$\frac{1}{4}$ is in lowest terms
1)	yellow			
2)	dark green			
3)	black			

31

More Families Of One-Color Trains

Cover the diagrams showing the one-color trains for dark green and blue. Then complete the tables for each color. Place each color on its family name row to determine the fraction using the family name. Then compare each color with the other one-color trains to find other possible names for the same fraction. Circle the fractions in lowest terms.

w	w	w	w	w	w
dark green					
green			green		
red		red		red	

w	w	w	w	w	w	w	w	w
blue								
green			green			green		

↓

1)

Dark green rod family (sixths)		
Rod color	Family name	Other names
red		
green		
purple		
yellow		

↓

2)

Blue rod family (ninths)		
Rod color	Family name	Other names
red		
green		
black		
dark green		

3) Build all the one-color trains for (orange & red) and fill in the table. Circle the fractions in lowest terms.

(Orange & red) rod family (twelfths)		
Rod color	Family name	Other names
red		
green		
purple		
dark green		
brown		
blue		
orange		

32

Introducing Addition Of Fractions With Rods

Cover the diagram on the left with rods to show the fractional parts of dark green. Note the white rods help to provide the family name for the dark green family.

w	w	w	w	w	w
dark green					
green			green		
red		red		red	

Rod color	Family names	Other names
white	$\frac{1}{6}$	none
red	$\frac{2}{6}$	$\frac{1}{3}$
green	$\frac{3}{6}$	$\frac{1}{2}$
purple	$\frac{4}{6}$	$\frac{2}{3}$
yellow	$\frac{5}{6}$	none
dark green	$\frac{6}{6}$	1

The rod patterns for dark green help us add fractions for halves, thirds, and sixths. For addition of fractions, rods are placed end-to-end, and then compared to the white rods in the dark green family.

Place a green and red rod end-to-end. Match with yellow to find the sum.

green		red
yellow		
w	w	w	w	w

Since yellow = 5 whites and each white = $\frac{1}{6}$, the answer is $\frac{5}{6}$.

Example I: $\frac{1}{2} + \frac{1}{3}$

green + red = yellow

$\frac{1}{2} + \frac{1}{3} = \left\langle \frac{5}{6} \right\rangle$

Place a red and white rod end-to-end. Match with green to find the sum.

red	w
green	
w	w	w

There are two possible answers. Green = 3 whites ($\frac{3}{6}$) or $\frac{1}{2}$. The answer in lowest terms is $\frac{1}{2}$.

Example II: $\frac{1}{3} + \frac{1}{6}$

red + white = 3 whites or green

$\frac{1}{3} + \frac{1}{6} = \left\langle \frac{3}{6} \right\rangle$ or $\left\langle \frac{1}{2} \right\rangle$

Use your rods to do these addition problems. Write the rod sentence on the blank lines below the problem. Write your fraction answers in the 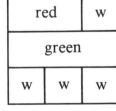 s. Put your anwers in lowest terms.

1) $\frac{1}{6} + \frac{2}{3} = \left\langle \right\rangle$

_____ + _____ = _____

2) $\frac{1}{2} + \frac{1}{6} = \left\langle \right\rangle$ or $\left\langle \right\rangle$

_____ + _____ = _____ or _____

Everything's Coming up Fractions with Cuisenaire Rods   © 1981 Cuisenaire Company of America, Inc.

Adding Fractions Using Rods

Cover the diagram below with rods to show the fractional parts of orange.

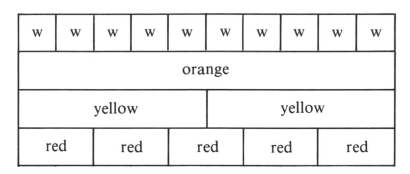

Use your rods to do each addition problem. Write the rod sentence on the blank lines below the problem. Write your fraction answers in the ⬡s. Put your answers in lowest terms.

Example: ⟨ $\frac{1}{2}$ ⟩ + ⟨ $\frac{1}{10}$ ⟩ = ⟨ $\frac{6}{10}$ ⟩ or ⟨ $\frac{3}{5}$ ⟩ ←Lowest terms express the fraction with the smallest possible numbers.

yellow + white = 6 whites or 3 reds

1) ⟨ $\frac{1}{2}$ ⟩ + ⟨ $\frac{1}{5}$ ⟩ = ⟨ ___ ⟩

_____ + _____ = _____

2) ⟨ $\frac{1}{5}$ ⟩ + ⟨ $\frac{7}{10}$ ⟩ = ⟨ ___ ⟩

_____ + _____ = _____

3) ⟨ $\frac{1}{2}$ ⟩ + ⟨ $\frac{3}{10}$ ⟩ = ⟨ ___ ⟩ or ⟨ ___ ⟩

_____ + _____ = _____ or _____

4) ⟨ $\frac{2}{5}$ ⟩ + ⟨ $\frac{1}{2}$ ⟩ = ⟨ ___ ⟩

_____ + _____ = _____

5) ⟨ $\frac{1}{10}$ ⟩ + ⟨ $\frac{1}{5}$ ⟩ = ⟨ ___ ⟩

_____ + _____ = _____

6) ⟨ $\frac{1}{5}$ ⟩ + ⟨ $\frac{3}{10}$ ⟩ = ⟨ ___ ⟩ or ⟨ ___ ⟩

_____ + _____ = _____ or _____

7) ⟨ $\frac{1}{10}$ ⟩ + ⟨ $\frac{3}{5}$ ⟩ = ⟨ ___ ⟩

_____ + _____ = _____

8) ⟨ $\frac{3}{10}$ ⟩ + ⟨ $\frac{1}{10}$ ⟩ = ⟨ ___ ⟩ or ⟨ ___ ⟩

_____ + _____ = _____ or _____

9) ⟨ $\frac{1}{10}$ ⟩ + ⟨ $\frac{1}{2}$ ⟩ = ⟨ ___ ⟩ or ⟨ ___ ⟩

_____ + _____ = _____ or _____

10) ⟨ $\frac{2}{5}$ ⟩ + ⟨ $\frac{1}{10}$ ⟩ = ⟨ ___ ⟩ or ⟨ ___ ⟩

_____ + _____ = _____ or _____

Everything's Coming up Fractions with Cuisenaire Rods   © 1981 Cuisenaire Company of America, Inc.

More Addition With The Rods

Cover the diagram below with rods to show the fractional parts of (orange & red).

w	w	w	w	w	w	w	w	w	w	w	w

orange		red

dark green	dark green

purple	purple	purple

green	green	green	green

red	red	red	red	red	red

Use your rods to do each addition problem. Write the rod sentence on the blank lines below the problem. Write your answers in the ⬡s. Put your answers in lowest terms.

1) $\left\langle\frac{1}{2}\right\rangle + \left\langle\frac{1}{12}\right\rangle = \left\langle\rule{1cm}{0.4pt}\right\rangle$

_____ + _____ = _____

2) $\left\langle\frac{1}{4}\right\rangle + \left\langle\frac{1}{6}\right\rangle = \left\langle\rule{1cm}{0.4pt}\right\rangle$

_____ + _____ = _____

3) $\left\langle\frac{1}{6}\right\rangle + \left\langle\frac{1}{12}\right\rangle = \left\langle\rule{0.6cm}{0.4pt}\right\rangle$ or $\left\langle\rule{0.6cm}{0.4pt}\right\rangle$

_____ + _____ = _____ or _____

4) $\left\langle\frac{5}{12}\right\rangle + \left\langle\frac{1}{6}\right\rangle = \left\langle\rule{1cm}{0.4pt}\right\rangle$

_____ + _____ = _____

5) $\left\langle\frac{1}{2}\right\rangle + \left\langle\frac{1}{6}\right\rangle = \left\langle\rule{0.6cm}{0.4pt}\right\rangle$ or $\left\langle\rule{0.6cm}{0.4pt}\right\rangle$ or $\left\langle\rule{0.6cm}{0.4pt}\right\rangle$

_____ + _____ = _____ or _____ or _____

6) $\left\langle\frac{1}{3}\right\rangle + \left\langle\frac{1}{12}\right\rangle = \left\langle\rule{1cm}{0.4pt}\right\rangle$

_____ + _____ = _____

7) $\left\langle\frac{1}{4}\right\rangle + \left\langle\frac{1}{3}\right\rangle = \left\langle\rule{1cm}{0.4pt}\right\rangle$

_____ + _____ = _____

8) $\left\langle\frac{5}{6}\right\rangle + \left\langle\frac{1}{12}\right\rangle = \left\langle\rule{1cm}{0.4pt}\right\rangle$

_____ + _____ = _____

9) $\left\langle\frac{1}{4}\right\rangle + \left\langle\frac{1}{12}\right\rangle = \left\langle\rule{0.6cm}{0.4pt}\right\rangle$ or $\left\langle\rule{0.6cm}{0.4pt}\right\rangle$ or $\left\langle\rule{0.6cm}{0.4pt}\right\rangle$

_____ + _____ = _____ or _____ or _____

10) $\left\langle\frac{2}{3}\right\rangle + \left\langle\frac{1}{12}\right\rangle = \left\langle\rule{0.6cm}{0.4pt}\right\rangle$ or $\left\langle\rule{0.6cm}{0.4pt}\right\rangle$

_____ + _____ = _____ or _____

35

Everything's Coming up Fractions with Cuisenaire Rods   © 1981 Cuisenaire Company of America, Inc.

RIDDLE I: What Coat Is Put On Only When Its Wet?

Make all the one-color trains for (orange & yellow). Use these trains to help solve the following problems. Match the letter given with each answer to solve the riddle. All answers have been expressed using the family name, fifteenths.

1) $\frac{1}{3} + \frac{1}{5} =$ ⬡ T

2) $\frac{1}{5} + \frac{1}{15} =$ ⬡ I

3) $\frac{2}{3} + \frac{1}{15} =$ ⬡ C

4) $\frac{3}{5} + \frac{1}{3} =$ ⬡ F

5) $\frac{1}{3} + \frac{1}{15} =$ ⬡ N

6) $\frac{2}{3} + \frac{1}{5} =$ ⬡ A

7) $\frac{2}{5} + \frac{1}{15} =$ ⬡ O

8) $\frac{4}{15} + \frac{2}{5} =$ ⬡ P

Riddle Answer

$\frac{13}{15}$		$\frac{11}{15}$	$\frac{7}{15}$	$\frac{13}{15}$	$\frac{8}{15}$		$\frac{7}{15}$	$\frac{14}{15}$		$\frac{10}{15}$	$\frac{13}{15}$	$\frac{4}{15}$	$\frac{6}{15}$	$\frac{8}{15}$

.

RIDDLE II: What Do You Say When You Call Your Dog And He Doesn't Come?

Make all the one-color trains for (orange & purple). Use these trains to help solve the following problems. Match the letter given with each answer to solve the riddle. All answers have been expressed using the family name, fourteenths.

1) $\frac{1}{2} + \frac{1}{7} =$ ⬡ N

2) $\frac{1}{7} + \frac{1}{14} =$ ⬡ E

3) $\frac{1}{2} + \frac{2}{7} =$ ⬡ O

4) $\frac{1}{2} + \frac{1}{14} =$ ⬡ G

5) $\frac{2}{7} + \frac{1}{14} =$ ⬡ D

6) $\frac{1}{2} + \frac{3}{7} =$ ⬡ !

Riddle Answer

$\frac{5}{14}$	$\frac{11}{14}$	$\frac{8}{14}$	$\frac{8}{14}$	$\frac{11}{14}$	$\frac{9}{14}$	$\frac{3}{14}$	$\frac{13}{14}$

36

RIDDLE: What Happens To Two Frogs Who Try To Catch The Same Bug At The Same Time?

Make all the one-color trains for (orange & dark green). Use these trains to help solve the following problems. Match the letter given with each answer to solve the riddle. All answers have been expressed using the family name, sixteenths.

1) $\frac{1}{2} + \frac{1}{8}$ = ⬡ U

2) $\frac{1}{2} + \frac{1}{16}$ = ⬡ E

3) $\frac{1}{4} + \frac{1}{16}$ = ⬡ U

4) $\frac{1}{2} + \frac{3}{8}$ = ⬡ O

5) $\frac{1}{2} + \frac{5}{16}$ = ⬡ Y

6) $\frac{1}{4} + \frac{3}{16}$ = ⬡ D

7) $\frac{1}{2} + \frac{1}{4}$ = ⬡ P

8) $\frac{1}{4} + \frac{1}{8}$ = ⬡ T

9) $\frac{1}{8} + \frac{1}{16}$ = ⬡ N

10) $\frac{1}{2} + \frac{3}{16}$ = ⬡ H

11) $\frac{5}{8} + \frac{5}{16}$ = ⬡ G

12) $\frac{1}{16} + \frac{7}{16}$ = ⬡ I

Riddle Answer

$\frac{6}{16}$	$\frac{11}{16}$	$\frac{9}{16}$	$\frac{13}{16}$

$\frac{9}{16}$	$\frac{3}{16}$	$\frac{7}{16}$

$\frac{5}{16}$	$\frac{12}{16}$

$\frac{6}{16}$	$\frac{14}{16}$	$\frac{3}{16}$	$\frac{15}{16}$	$\frac{10}{16}$	$\frac{9}{16}$

$\frac{6}{16}$	$\frac{8}{16}$	$\frac{9}{16}$	$\frac{7}{16}$

Everything's Coming up Fractions with Cuisenaire Rods   © 1981 Cuisenaire Company of America, Inc.

RIDDLE: What's The Difference Between A Man Going Up The Stairs And A Man Looking Up The Stairs?

Make all the one-color trains for (orange & brown). Use these trains to help solve the following problems. Match the letter given with each answer to solve the riddle. All answers have been expressed using the family name, eighteenths.

1) $\frac{1}{2} + \frac{1}{3}$ = 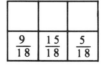 N

2) $\frac{1}{2} + \frac{1}{9}$ = 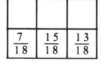 P

3) $\frac{1}{9} + \frac{1}{6}$ = 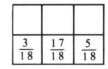 E

4) $\frac{1}{3} + \frac{1}{18}$ = 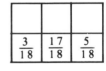 A

5) $\frac{1}{6} + \frac{1}{18}$ = S

6) $\frac{5}{6} + \frac{1}{9}$ = H

7) $\frac{1}{2} + \frac{1}{6}$ = R

8) $\frac{1}{2} + \frac{1}{18}$ = 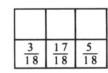 U

9) $\frac{1}{3} + \frac{1}{9}$ = 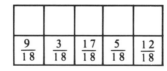 I

10) $\frac{1}{6} + \frac{1}{3}$ = 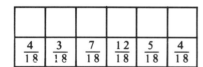 O

11) $\frac{1}{9} + \frac{1}{18}$ = 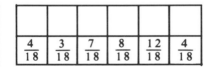 T

12) $\frac{1}{2} + \frac{2}{9}$ = 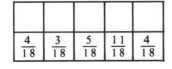 D

Riddle Answer

$\frac{9}{18}$	$\frac{15}{18}$	$\frac{5}{18}$

$\frac{4}{18}$	$\frac{3}{18}$	$\frac{5}{18}$	$\frac{11}{18}$	$\frac{4}{18}$

$\frac{10}{18}$	$\frac{11}{18}$

$\frac{3}{18}$	$\frac{17}{18}$	$\frac{5}{18}$

$\frac{4}{18}$	$\frac{3}{18}$	$\frac{7}{18}$	$\frac{8}{18}$	$\frac{12}{18}$	$\frac{4}{18}$

$\frac{7}{18}$	$\frac{15}{18}$	$\frac{13}{18}$

$\frac{3}{18}$	$\frac{17}{18}$	$\frac{5}{18}$

$\frac{9}{18}$	$\frac{3}{18}$	$\frac{17}{18}$	$\frac{5}{18}$	$\frac{12}{18}$

$\frac{4}{18}$	$\frac{3}{18}$	$\frac{7}{18}$	$\frac{12}{18}$	$\frac{5}{18}$	$\frac{4}{18}$

$\frac{10}{18}$	$\frac{11}{18}$

$\frac{3}{18}$	$\frac{17}{18}$	$\frac{5}{18}$

$\frac{4}{18}$	$\frac{3}{18}$	$\frac{5}{18}$	$\frac{11}{18}$	$\frac{4}{18}$

Everything's Coming up Fractions with Cuisenaire Rods © 1981 Cuisenaire Company of America, Inc.

Using Common Denominators To Add Fractions

w	w	w	w	w	w	w	w	w	w
orange									
yellow					yellow				
red		red		red		red		red	

The rod patterns for orange show that the family name (common denominator) for halves, fifths, and tenths is tenths. We can use this common denominator to add fractions.

Example:

$\frac{1}{2} = \boxed{\frac{5}{10}}$ ← Change each fraction to its family name (common denominator).

$+ \frac{1}{5} = \boxed{\frac{2}{10}}$ ←

$\boxed{\frac{7}{10}}$ ← Then add.

Check your answer by using rods:

$\frac{1}{2}$ of orange = yellow = 5 whites ($\frac{5}{10}$)

$\frac{1}{5}$ of orange = red = 2 whites ($\frac{2}{10}$)

yellow + red = black = 7 whites ($\frac{7}{10}$)

Solve the following addition problems by finding a common denominator. Put answers in lowest terms. Check all problems with rods.

1) $\frac{1}{2} = \langle - \rangle$

$+ \frac{2}{5} = \langle - \rangle$

$\langle - \rangle$

2) $\frac{1}{2} = \langle - \rangle$

$+ \frac{1}{10} = \langle - \rangle$

$\langle - \rangle$ or $\langle - \rangle$

3) $\frac{2}{5} = \langle - \rangle$

$+ \frac{1}{10} = \langle - \rangle$

$\langle - \rangle$ or $\langle - \rangle$

4) $\frac{2}{5} = \langle - \rangle$

$+ \frac{3}{10} = \langle - \rangle$

$\langle - \rangle$

5) $\frac{1}{5} = \langle - \rangle$

$+ \frac{1}{10} = \langle - \rangle$

$\langle - \rangle$

6) $\frac{1}{2} = \langle - \rangle$

$+ \frac{3}{10} = \langle - \rangle$

$\langle - \rangle$ or $\langle - \rangle$

39

RIDDLE: What Has One Horn, Runs Up And Down The Street, And Gives Milk?

w	w	w	w	w	w	w	w	w	w	w	w	w	w	w

orange		yellow

yellow	yellow	yellow

green	green	green	green	green

Cover the diagram to show the fractional parts of (orange & yellow). Solve the following addition problems by finding a common denominator. Put answers in lowest terms. Check all problems with rods. Match each answer with the letter to solve the riddle.

1) $\frac{1}{3}$ = ⬡
   $+ \frac{1}{5}$ = ⬡
   _____ R
   ⬡

2) $\frac{1}{3}$ = ⬡
   $+ \frac{2}{5}$ = ⬡
   _____ K
   ⬡

3) $\frac{2}{3}$ = ⬡
   $+ \frac{1}{5}$ = ⬡
   _____ A
   ⬡

4) $\frac{3}{5}$ = ⬡
   $+ \frac{1}{3}$ = ⬡
   _____ I
   ⬡

5) $\frac{1}{3}$ = ⬡
   $+ \frac{1}{15}$ = ⬡
   _____ L
   ⬡ or ⬡

6) $\frac{1}{5}$ = ⬡
   $+ \frac{7}{15}$ = ⬡
   _____ C
   ⬡ or ⬡

7) $\frac{4}{15}$ = ⬡
   $+ \frac{1}{3}$ = ⬡
   _____ T
   ⬡ or ⬡

8) $\frac{2}{5}$ = ⬡
   $+ \frac{1}{15}$ = ⬡
   _____ U
   ⬡

9) $\frac{2}{3}$ = ⬡
   $+ \frac{2}{15}$ = ⬡
   _____ M
   ⬡ or ⬡

Riddle Answer

$\frac{13}{15}$		$\frac{4}{5}$	$\frac{14}{15}$	$\frac{2}{5}$	$\frac{11}{15}$		$\frac{3}{5}$	$\frac{8}{15}$	$\frac{7}{15}$	$\frac{2}{3}$	$\frac{11}{15}$

40

Addition Problems With Sums Greater Than One

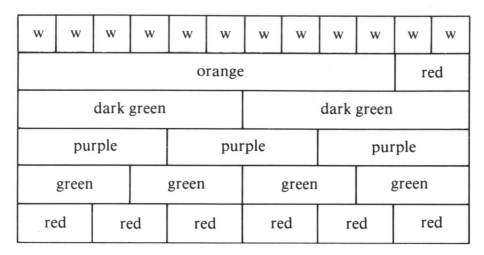

When fractions are added, the answer (sum) may be greater than one.

Example:

$$\frac{3}{4} = \frac{9}{12}$$
$$+ \frac{1}{3} = \frac{4}{12}$$
$$\overline{\qquad}$$
$$\frac{13}{12}$$

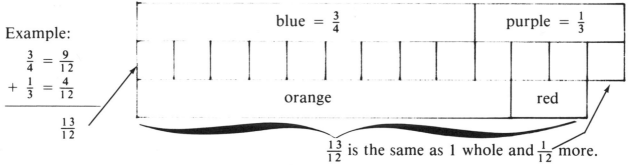

blue = $\frac{3}{4}$ purple = $\frac{1}{3}$

orange   red

$\frac{13}{12}$ is the same as 1 whole and $\frac{1}{12}$ more.

The mixed number for $\frac{13}{12}$ is written as $1\frac{1}{12}$.

Solve the following addition problems using a common denominator. Convert your answer to a mixed number. Check by using rods.

1) $\frac{7}{12} = \bigcirc$
   $+ \frac{5}{6} = \bigcirc$
   $\bigcirc$
   or

2) $\frac{3}{4} = \bigcirc$
   $+ \frac{2}{3} = \bigcirc$
   $\bigcirc$
   or

3) $\frac{5}{12} = \bigcirc$
   $+ \frac{2}{3} = \bigcirc$
   $\bigcirc$
   or

4) $\frac{5}{6} = \bigcirc$
   $+ \frac{3}{4} = \bigcirc$
   $\bigcirc$
   or

Mixed
Numbers _____   _____   _____   _____

41

Everything's Coming up Fractions with Cuisenaire Rods   © 1981 Cuisenaire Company of America, Inc.

Introducing Subtraction Of Fractions With Rods

Cover the diagram on the left below with rods to show the fractional parts of brown. Note the white rods help to provide the family name for the brown family.

w	w	w	w	w	w	w	w
brown							
purple				purple			
red		red		red		red	

Rod color	Family name	Other names
white	$\frac{1}{8}$	none
red	$\frac{2}{8}$	$\frac{1}{4}$
green	$\frac{3}{8}$	none
purple	$\frac{4}{8}$	$\frac{1}{2}$
yellow	$\frac{5}{8}$	none
dark green	$\frac{6}{8}$	$\frac{3}{4}$
black	$\frac{7}{8}$	none
brown	$\frac{8}{8}$	1

The rod patterns for brown help us to subtract fractions for halves, fourths, and eighths. For subtraction of fractions, rods are placed side-by-side.

Example 1:

$$\frac{7}{8} - \frac{1}{4}$$

black − red = yellow

$$\frac{7}{8} - \frac{1}{4} = \left\langle \frac{5}{8} \right\rangle$$

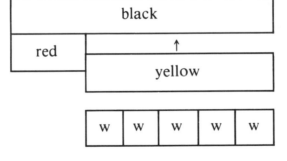

Place a black and a red rod side-by-side. The difference is yellow. Since yellow = 5 whites and each white = $\frac{1}{8}$, the answer is $\frac{5}{8}$.

Example 2:

$$\frac{1}{2} - \frac{1}{8}$$

purple − white = green

$$\frac{1}{2} - \frac{1}{8} = \left\langle \frac{3}{8} \right\rangle$$

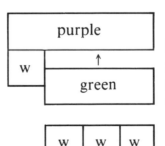

Place a purple and a white rod side-by-side. The difference is green. Green = 3 whites ($\frac{3}{8}$).

Use your rods to do these subtraction problems. Write the rod sentence on the blank lines below the problem. Write your fraction answers in the ⟨——⟩ s.

1) $\frac{5}{8} - \frac{1}{4} = \left\langle —— \right\rangle$

_____ − _____ = _____

2) $\frac{7}{8} - \frac{1}{2} = \left\langle —— \right\rangle$

_____ − _____ = _____

3) $\frac{7}{8} - \frac{3}{4} = \left\langle —— \right\rangle$

_____ − _____ = _____

42

Subtracting Fractions Using Rods

Cover the diagram below with rods to show the fractional parts of dark green.

w	w	w	w	w	w
dark green					
green			green		
red		red		red	

Use your rods to do each subtraction problem. Write the rod sentence on the blank lines below the problem. Write your fraction answers in the ⬡ s. Put your answers in lowest terms.

Example: ⟨$\frac{1}{2}$⟩ − ⟨$\frac{1}{6}$⟩ = ⟨$\frac{2}{6}$⟩ or ⟨$\frac{1}{3}$⟩ ←Lowest terms express the fraction with the smallest possible numbers.

<u>green</u> − <u>white</u> = <u>2 whites</u> or <u>red</u>

1) ⟨$\frac{1}{2}$⟩ − ⟨$\frac{1}{3}$⟩ = ⟨——⟩

_____ − _____ = _____

2) ⟨$\frac{1}{3}$⟩ − ⟨$\frac{1}{6}$⟩ = ⟨——⟩

_____ − _____ = _____

3) ⟨$\frac{2}{3}$⟩ − ⟨$\frac{1}{2}$⟩ = ⟨——⟩

_____ − _____ = _____

4) ⟨$\frac{2}{3}$⟩ − ⟨$\frac{1}{6}$⟩ = ⟨——⟩ or ⟨——⟩

_____ − _____ = _____ or _____

5) ⟨$\frac{5}{6}$⟩ − ⟨$\frac{1}{3}$⟩ = ⟨——⟩ or ⟨——⟩

_____ − _____ = _____ or _____

6) ⟨$\frac{1}{2}$⟩ − ⟨$\frac{1}{6}$⟩ = ⟨——⟩ or ⟨——⟩

_____ − _____ = _____ or _____

7) ⟨$\frac{5}{6}$⟩ − ⟨$\frac{1}{2}$⟩ = ⟨——⟩ or ⟨——⟩

_____ − _____ = _____ or _____

8) ⟨$\frac{5}{6}$⟩ − ⟨$\frac{2}{3}$⟩ = ⟨——⟩

_____ − _____ = _____

43

More Subtraction With Rods

Cover the diagram below with rods to show the fractional parts of brown.

w	w	w	w	w	w	w	w
brown								
purple				purple			
red		red		red		red	

Use your rods to do each subtraction problem. Write the rod sentence on the blank lines below the problem. Write your fraction answers in the ⬡ s. Put your answers in lowest terms.

1) $\langle \frac{1}{2} \rangle - \langle \frac{1}{4} \rangle = \bigcirc$ or $\bigcirc$

_____ − _____ = _____ or _____

2) $\langle \frac{1}{2} \rangle - \langle \frac{1}{8} \rangle = \bigcirc$

_____ − _____ = _____

3) $\langle \frac{3}{4} \rangle - \langle \frac{1}{2} \rangle = \bigcirc$ or $\bigcirc$

_____ − _____ = _____ or _____

4) $\langle \frac{3}{4} \rangle - \langle \frac{1}{8} \rangle = \bigcirc$

_____ − _____ = _____

5) $\langle \frac{3}{8} \rangle - \langle \frac{1}{4} \rangle = \bigcirc$

_____ − _____ = _____

6) $\langle \frac{5}{8} \rangle - \langle \frac{1}{2} \rangle = \bigcirc$

_____ − _____ = _____

7) $\langle \frac{7}{8} \rangle - \langle \frac{1}{4} \rangle = \bigcirc$

_____ − _____ = _____

8) $\langle \frac{7}{8} \rangle - \langle \frac{3}{4} \rangle = \bigcirc$

_____ − _____ = _____

9) $\langle \frac{5}{8} \rangle - \langle \frac{1}{4} \rangle = \bigcirc$

_____ − _____ = _____

10) $\langle \frac{3}{4} \rangle - \langle \frac{5}{8} \rangle = \bigcirc$

_____ − _____ = _____

11) $\langle 1 \rangle - \langle \frac{1}{4} \rangle = \bigcirc$ or $\bigcirc$

_____ − _____ = _____ or _____

12) $\langle 1 \rangle - \langle \frac{3}{8} \rangle = \bigcirc$

_____ − _____ = _____

44

Everything's Coming up Fractions with Cuisenaire Rods   © 1981 Cuisenaire Company of America, Inc.

RIDDLE: What's The Difference Between An Angry Rabbit And A Counterfeit $10 Bill?

Make all the one-color trains for (orange & brown). Use these trains to help solve the following problems. Match the letter given with each answer to solve the riddle. All answers have been expressed using the family name, eighteenths.

1) $\frac{1}{2} - \frac{1}{9} =$ 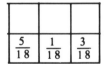 Y

2) $\frac{1}{2} - \frac{1}{18} =$ 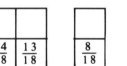 A

3) $\frac{1}{3} - \frac{1}{9} =$ T

4) $\frac{1}{3} - \frac{1}{18} =$ O

5) $\frac{1}{6} - \frac{1}{9} =$ 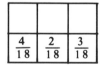 N

6) $\frac{2}{3} - \frac{1}{9} =$ M

7) $\frac{2}{3} - \frac{1}{18} =$ B

8) $\frac{5}{6} - \frac{1}{9} =$ S

9) $\frac{5}{6} - \frac{1}{18} =$ 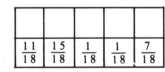 I

10) $\frac{8}{9} - \frac{1}{18} =$ 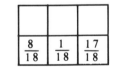 U

11) $\frac{7}{9} - \frac{2}{3} =$ 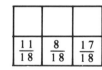 H

12) $\frac{4}{9} - \frac{5}{18} =$ E

13) $\frac{1}{2} - \frac{1}{6} =$ R

14) $1 - \frac{1}{18} =$ 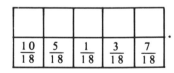 D

Riddle Answer

$\frac{5}{18}$	$\frac{1}{18}$	$\frac{3}{18}$

$\frac{14}{18}$	$\frac{13}{18}$

$\frac{8}{18}$

$\frac{10}{18}$	$\frac{8}{18}$	$\frac{17}{18}$

$\frac{11}{18}$	$\frac{15}{18}$	$\frac{1}{18}$	$\frac{1}{18}$	$\frac{7}{18}$

$\frac{8}{18}$	$\frac{1}{18}$	$\frac{17}{18}$

$\frac{4}{18}$	$\frac{2}{18}$	$\frac{3}{18}$

$\frac{5}{18}$	$\frac{4}{18}$	$\frac{2}{18}$	$\frac{3}{18}$	$\frac{6}{18}$

$\frac{14}{18}$	$\frac{13}{18}$

$\frac{11}{18}$	$\frac{8}{18}$	$\frac{17}{18}$

$\frac{10}{18}$	$\frac{5}{18}$	$\frac{1}{18}$	$\frac{3}{18}$	$\frac{7}{18}$

Everything's Coming up Fractions with Cuisenaire Rods   © 1981 Cuisenaire Company of America, Inc.

Using Common Denominators To Subtract Fractions

w	w	w	w	w	w	w	w	w	w	w	w

| orange | | | | | | | | | | red | |

| dark green | | | | | | dark green | | | | | |

| purple | | | purple | | | purple | | | | | |

| green | | green | | green | | green | | | | | |

| red | | red | | red | | red | | red | | red | |

The rod patterns for (orange & red) show that the family name (common denominator) for halves, thirds, fourths, sixths, and twelfths is twelfths. We can use this common denominator to subtract fractions.

Example:

1) $\frac{1}{3} = \left\langle \frac{4}{12} \right\rangle$ ← Change each fraction to its family name (common denominator).

$-\frac{1}{4} = \left\langle \frac{3}{12} \right\rangle$ ←

$\left\langle \frac{1}{12} \right\rangle$ ←Then subtract

Check your answer by using rods:

$\frac{1}{3}$ of orange = purple = 4 whites ($\frac{4}{12}$)

$\frac{1}{4}$ of orange = green = 3 whites ($\frac{3}{12}$)

purple – green = white ($\frac{1}{12}$)

Solve the following subtraction problems by finding a common denominator. Put answers in lowest terms. Check all problems with rods.

1) $\frac{1}{6} = \left\langle - \right\rangle$

$-\frac{1}{12} = \left\langle - \right\rangle$

$\left\langle - \right\rangle$

2) $\frac{1}{4} = \left\langle - \right\rangle$

$-\frac{1}{6} = \left\langle - \right\rangle$

$\left\langle - \right\rangle$

3) $\frac{3}{4} = \left\langle - \right\rangle$

$-\frac{1}{3} = \left\langle - \right\rangle$

$\left\langle - \right\rangle$

4) $\frac{5}{6} = \left\langle - \right\rangle$

$-\frac{1}{4} = \left\langle - \right\rangle$

$\left\langle - \right\rangle$

5) $\frac{5}{6} = \left\langle - \right\rangle$

$-\frac{7}{12} = \left\langle - \right\rangle$

$\left\langle - \right\rangle$ or $\left\langle - \right\rangle$

6) $\frac{3}{4} = \left\langle - \right\rangle$

$-\frac{5}{12} = \left\langle - \right\rangle$

$\left\langle - \right\rangle$ or $\left\langle - \right\rangle$

Everything's Coming up Fractions with Cuisenaire Rods   © 1981 Cuisenaire Company of America, Inc.

Using Common Denominators To Subtract Fractions

w	w	w	w	w	w	w	w	w	w	w	w	w	w	w	w

| orange | | | | | | | | | | dark green | | | | | |

| brown | | | | | | | | brown | | | | | | | |

| purple | | | | purple | | | | purple | | | | purple | | | |

| red | | red | | red | | red | | red | | red | | red | | red | |

Cover the diagram to show the fractional parts of (orange & dark green). Solve the following subtraction problems by finding a common denominator. Check all problems with the rods.

1) $\frac{5}{16}$ = ⬡
   $-\frac{1}{4}$ = ⬡
   _____
   ⬡

2) $\frac{5}{8}$ = ⬡
   $-\frac{3}{16}$ = ⬡
   _____
   ⬡

3) $\frac{3}{4}$ = ⬡
   $-\frac{1}{16}$ = ⬡
   _____
   ⬡

4) $\frac{1}{2}$ = ⬡
   $-\frac{3}{16}$ = ⬡
   _____
   ⬡

5) $\frac{7}{8}$ = ⬡
   $-\frac{5}{16}$ = ⬡
   _____
   ⬡

6) $\frac{9}{16}$ = ⬡
   $-\frac{3}{8}$ = ⬡
   _____
   ⬡

7) $\frac{15}{16}$ = ⬡
   $-\frac{1}{2}$ = ⬡
   _____
   ⬡

8) $\frac{3}{4}$ = ⬡
   $-\frac{7}{16}$ = ⬡
   _____
   ⬡

9) $\frac{15}{16}$ = ⬡
   $-\frac{1}{8}$ = ⬡
   _____
   ⬡

Everything's Coming up Fractions with Cuisenaire Rods   © 1981 Cuisenaire Company of America, Inc.

RIDDLE: What Has A Foot At Each End And A Foot In The Middle?

| w | w | w | w | w | w | w | w | w | w | w | w |

orange		red
dark green		dark green
purple	purple	purple
green	green	green	green
red	red	red	red	red	red

Cover the diagram to show fractional parts of (orange & red). Solve the following addition and subtraction problems by using the family name (common denominator). Express all final answers in lowest terms. Match each answer with the given letter to solve the riddle.

1) $\frac{5}{12}$ = ⬡
 + $\frac{1}{4}$ = ⬡
 ———————
 ⬡ or ⬡   D

2) $\frac{1}{4}$ = ⬡
 − $\frac{1}{6}$ = ⬡
 ———————
 ⬡   I

3) $\frac{1}{4}$ = ⬡
 + $\frac{1}{6}$ = ⬡
 ———————
 ⬡   T

4) $\frac{5}{6}$ = ⬡
 − $\frac{1}{4}$ = ⬡
 ———————
 ⬡   C

5) $\frac{2}{3}$ = ⬡
 + $\frac{1}{4}$ = ⬡
 ———————
 ⬡   Y

6) $\frac{5}{12}$ = ⬡
 − $\frac{1}{4}$ = ⬡
 ———————
 ⬡ or ⬡   K

7) $\frac{1}{12}$ = ⬡
 + $\frac{1}{6}$ = ⬡
 ———————
 ⬡ or ⬡   S

8) $\frac{5}{6}$ = ⬡
 − $\frac{1}{2}$ = ⬡
 ———————
 ⬡ or ⬡   R

9) $\frac{2}{3}$ = ⬡
 + $\frac{1}{12}$ = ⬡
 ———————
 ⬡ or ⬡   A

Riddle Answer

| $\frac{3}{4}$ | | $\frac{11}{12}$ | $\frac{3}{4}$ | $\frac{1}{3}$ | $\frac{2}{3}$ | $\frac{1}{4}$ | $\frac{5}{12}$ | $\frac{1}{12}$ | $\frac{7}{12}$ | $\frac{1}{6}$ |

Everything's Coming up Fractions with Cuisenaire Rods   © 1981 Cuisenaire Company of America, Inc.

RIDDLE: What Happens To A Dog Who Eats Table Scraps?

Make the one-color trains for (orange & brown). Solve the following addition and subtraction problems by using the family name (common denominator). Express all final answers in lowest terms. Match each answer with the given letter to solve the riddle.

Add

1) $\frac{1}{2} = \bigcirc$
$+ \frac{5}{18} = \bigcirc$
——————
$\bigcirc$ or $\bigcirc$ G

2) $\frac{1}{2} = \bigcirc$
$+ \frac{4}{9} = \bigcirc$
——————
$\bigcirc$ P

3) $\frac{5}{6} = \bigcirc$
$+ \frac{1}{18} = \bigcirc$
——————
$\bigcirc$ or $\bigcirc$ T

4) $\frac{4}{9} = \bigcirc$
$+ \frac{1}{6} = \bigcirc$
——————
$\bigcirc$ N

5) $\frac{2}{9} = \bigcirc$
$+ \frac{5}{18} = \bigcirc$
——————
$\bigcirc$ or $\bigcirc$ E

6) $\frac{1}{6} = \bigcirc$
$+ \frac{7}{18} = \bigcirc$
——————
$\bigcirc$ or $\bigcirc$ R

Subtract

7) $\frac{8}{9} = \bigcirc$
$- \frac{1}{2} = \bigcirc$
——————
$\bigcirc$ H

8) $\frac{5}{6} = \bigcirc$
$- \frac{2}{3} = \bigcirc$
——————
$\bigcirc$ or $\bigcirc$ I

9) $\frac{1}{2} = \bigcirc$
$- \frac{4}{9} = \bigcirc$
——————
$\bigcirc$ S

10) $\frac{2}{3} = \bigcirc$
$- \frac{7}{18} = \bigcirc$
——————
$\bigcirc$ U

11) $\frac{5}{6} = \bigcirc$
$- \frac{1}{9} = \bigcirc$
——————
$\bigcirc$ L

12) $\frac{11}{18} = \bigcirc$
$- \frac{1}{2} = \bigcirc$
——————
$\bigcirc$ or $\bigcirc$ O

Riddle Answer

$\frac{7}{18}$	$\frac{1}{2}$

$\frac{7}{9}$	$\frac{1}{2}$	$\frac{8}{9}$	$\frac{1}{18}$

$\frac{1}{18}$	$\frac{17}{18}$	$\frac{13}{18}$	$\frac{1}{6}$	$\frac{11}{18}$	$\frac{8}{9}$	$\frac{1}{2}$	$\frac{5}{9}$	$\frac{1}{18}$

$\frac{1}{6}$	$\frac{11}{18}$

$\frac{7}{18}$	$\frac{1}{6}$	$\frac{1}{18}$

$\frac{8}{9}$	$\frac{1}{9}$	$\frac{11}{18}$	$\frac{7}{9}$	$\frac{5}{18}$	$\frac{1}{2}$

Everything's Coming up Fractions with Cuisenaire Rods © 1981 Cuisenaire Company of America, Inc.

Answers and Commentary

Page 1: 1) green 2) yellow 3) brown 4) orange 5) dark green 6) blue 7) purple 8) black 9) red

Page 2: 4) (A) 5) (C) 6) (B)

Page 3: 1) (B) 2) (A) 3) (C) 4) (E) 5) (D)

Page 4: 1) True, T 2) False, A 3) True, W 4) False, B 5) False, N 6) True, I 7) False, U 8) True, F
9) False, D 10) True, L 11) False, C 12) True, S 13) False, H 14) False, O 15) True, E

B	E	C	A	U	S	E		T	H	E	N		I	T		W	O	U	L	D
4	15	11	2	7	12	15		1	13	15	5		6	1		3	14	7	10	9

B	E		A		F	O	O	T
4	15		2		8	14	14	1

Page 5: 4) (A) 5) (B) 6) (D) 7) (C)

Page 6: 1) (A) 2) (D) 3) (B) 4) (C) 5) (G) 6) (F) 7) (E) 8) (H)

Page 7: 1) True, Y 2) False, F 3) False, C 4) True, O 5) False, H 6) False, L 7) True, T 8) True, M
9) True, P 10) True, R 11) True, I 12) False, S 13) True, U 14) False, A 15) True, E 16) True, N

O	N	L	Y		O	N	E		A	F	T	E	R		T	H	A	T
4	16	6	1		4	16	15		14	2	7	15	10		7	5	14	7

Y	O	U	R		S	T	O	M	A	C	H		I	S		N	O	T		E	M	P	T	Y	.
1	4	13	10		12	7	4	8	14	3	5		11	12		16	4	7		15	8	9	7	1	

Page 8: 1) (B) 2) (A) 3) (C) 4) (D) 5) (F) 6) (E) 7) (G) 8) (H)

Page 9: 1) True, S 2) True, L 3) True, O 4) False, M 5) False, E 6) False, R 7) False, T 8) True, F
9) True, N 10) False, P 10) True, H 12) False, A

O	N	E		S	T	E	A	L	S		F	R	O	M		T	H	E
3	9	5		1	7	5	12	2	1		8	6	3	4		7	11	5

P	E	O	P	L	E	;	T	H	E		O	T	H	E	R		P	E	A	L	S
10	5	3	10	2	5		7	11	5		3	7	11	5	6		10	5	12	2	1

F	R	O	M		T	H	E		S	T	E	E	P	L	E	.
8	6	3	4		7	11	5		1	7	5	5	10	2	5	

Page 10: 1) a) 3 b) 9   2) a) 2 b) 4 c) 8   3) a) 2 b) 5 c) 10

Page 11: 1) a) 2 red b) white white   2) a) 7 white   3) a) 2 green b) red red c) 6 white

Page 12: 1) a) yellow 2 $\frac{1}{2}$ yellow
  b) red 5 $\frac{1}{5}$ red
  c) white 10 $\frac{1}{10}$ white

2) Answers may be given in any order.
  a) dark green 2 $\frac{1}{2}$ dark green
  b) purple 3 $\frac{1}{3}$ purple
  c) green 4 $\frac{1}{4}$ green
  d) red 6 $\frac{1}{6}$ red
  e) white 12 $\frac{1}{12}$ white

50

Page 13:
1) Answers may be given in any order.

$\frac{1}{2}$ black

$\frac{1}{7}$ red

$\frac{1}{14}$ white

2) Answers may be given in any order.

$\frac{1}{3}$ yellow

$\frac{1}{5}$ green

$\frac{1}{15}$ white

3) Answers may be given in any order.

$\frac{1}{2}$ brown

$\frac{1}{4}$ purple

$\frac{1}{8}$ red

$\frac{1}{16}$ white

Page 14:
1) Answers may be given in any order.

$\frac{1}{2}$ blue

$\frac{1}{3}$ dark green

$\frac{1}{6}$ green

$\frac{1}{9}$ red

$\frac{1}{18}$ white

2)

     orange

     yellow

     purple

     red

     white

3) Answers may be given in any order.

$\frac{1}{3}$ black

$\frac{1}{7}$ green

$\frac{1}{21}$ white

Page 15:
1) <u>Red</u> is $\frac{1}{4}$ of brown.

2) <u>White</u> is $\frac{1}{3}$ of green.

3) Purple is $\frac{1}{3}$ of (orange & <u>red</u>).

4) <u>Red</u> is $\frac{1}{5}$ of orange.

5) Green is $\frac{1}{6}$ of (orange & <u>brown</u>).

6) <u>Brown</u> is $\frac{1}{2}$ of (orange & dark green).

7) Dark green is $\frac{1}{3}$ of (orange & <u>brown</u>).

8) White is $\frac{1}{7}$ of <u>black</u>.

9) <u>Black</u> is $\frac{1}{3}$ of (orange & orange & white).

10) Red is $\frac{1}{6}$ of (orange & <u>red</u>).

11) <u>Green</u> is $\frac{1}{5}$ of (orange & yellow).

12) White is $\frac{1}{9}$ of <u>blue</u>.

Page 16:
1) W (white)
2) P (purple)
3) R (red)
4) O̶ (orange)
5) D (dark green)
6) O̶ (orange)
7) E (blue)
8) W (white)
9) R (red)
10) P (purple)
11) E (blue)
12) E (blue)
13) K (black)
14) D (dark green)
15) R (red)
16) O̶ (orange)
17) P (purple)
18) D (dark green)
19) Y (yellow)
20) E (blue)
21) G (green)
22) R (red)
23) O̶ (orange)
24) W (white)

Crossword Answers

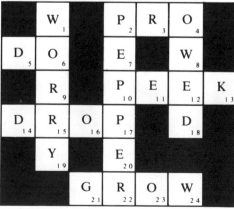

Page 17: 1) two reds   2) three reds   3) three whites

Page 18: 1) two greens   2) five whites   3) three whites

4) six whites   5) two purples   6) three greens

Everything's Coming up Fractions with Cuisenaire Rods   © 1981 Cuisenaire Company of America, Inc.

Page 19: 1) $\frac{1}{2}$ 2) $\frac{2}{3}$ 3) $\frac{3}{4}$ 4) $\frac{5}{6}$ 5) $\frac{7}{12}$

6) $\frac{1}{2}$ 7) $\frac{3}{7}$ 8) $\frac{5}{14}$

	Table I					Table II			Riddle Answer
Prob. No.	4	1	5	3	2	8	7	6	T H E M A N E P A R T
Letter	M	P	H	R	N	E	A	T	

Page 20: 1) G (green) 5) Ơ (orange)

2) W (white) 6) P (purple)

3) R (red) 7) D (dark green)

4) E (blue) 8) N (brown)

9) - 16)

	Table II								Riddle Answer
Problem No.	9	16	12	15	14	13	11	10	A H I L L I S H A R D T O G E T U P .
Letter	A	P	I	T	S	L	H	U	A P I L L I S H A R D T O G E T D O W N .

Page 21: 1) Green matches green ($\frac{1}{2}$) and three whites ($\frac{3}{6}$).

2) Red matches red ($\frac{1}{3}$) and two whites ($\frac{2}{6}$).

3) Purple matches two reds ($\frac{2}{3}$) and four whites ($\frac{4}{6}$).

4) Yellow matches five whites ($\frac{5}{6}$).

Page 22: 1) $\frac{4}{7}$ 2) $\frac{2}{5}$ $\frac{4}{10}$ 3) $\frac{1}{3}$ $\frac{2}{6}$ $\frac{4}{12}$

Page 23: 1) $\frac{3}{4}$ $\frac{6}{8}$ 2) $\frac{2}{3}$ $\frac{6}{9}$ 3) $\frac{6}{7}$ 4) $\frac{3}{7}$ $\frac{6}{14}$

Page 24: 1) Purple matches purple ($\frac{1}{3}$), two reds ($\frac{2}{6}$), and four whites ($\frac{4}{12}$).

2) Green matches green ($\frac{1}{4}$) and three whites ($\frac{3}{12}$).

3) Red matches red ($\frac{1}{6}$) and two whites ($\frac{2}{12}$)

4) White matches white ($\frac{1}{12}$).

5) Yellow matches five whites ($\frac{5}{12}$)

6) Black matches seven whites ($\frac{7}{12}$)

7) Brown matches two purples ($\frac{2}{3}$), four reds ($\frac{4}{6}$), and eight whites ($\frac{8}{12}$).

8) Blue matches three greens ($\frac{3}{4}$) and nine whites ($\frac{9}{12}$).

9) Orange matches five reds ($\frac{5}{6}$) and ten whites ($\frac{10}{12}$).

10) (Orange & white) matches eleven whites ($\frac{11}{12}$).

Page 25: I

1) Red matches red ($\frac{1}{5}$) and two whites ($\frac{2}{10}$).

2) Green matches three whites ($\frac{3}{10}$).

3) Purple matches two reds ($\frac{2}{5}$) and four whites ($\frac{4}{10}$).

4) Yellow matches one yellow ($\frac{1}{2}$) and five whites ($\frac{5}{10}$).

5) Dark green matches three reds ($\frac{3}{5}$) and six whites ($\frac{6}{10}$).

6) Brown matches four reds ($\frac{4}{5}$) and eight whites ($\frac{8}{10}$).

7) Blue matches nine whites ($\frac{9}{10}$).

8) Red matches red ($\frac{1}{9}$) and two whites ($\frac{2}{18}$).

9) Green matches green ($\frac{1}{6}$) and three whites ($\frac{3}{18}$).

10) Purple matches two reds ($\frac{2}{9}$) and four whites ($\frac{4}{18}$).

11) Yellow matches five whites ($\frac{5}{18}$).

52

12) Dark green matches dark green ($\frac{1}{3}$), two greens ($\frac{2}{6}$), three reds ($\frac{3}{9}$) and six whites ($\frac{6}{18}$).

13) Blue matches blue ($\frac{1}{2}$), three greens ($\frac{3}{6}$), and nine whites ($\frac{9}{18}$).

14) Orange matches five reds ($\frac{5}{9}$) or ten whites ($\frac{10}{18}$).

15) (Orange & red) matches two dark greens ($\frac{2}{3}$), four greens ($\frac{4}{6}$), six reds ($\frac{6}{9}$), and twelve whites ($\frac{12}{18}$).

16) (Orange & purple) matches seven reds ($\frac{7}{9}$) and fourteen whites ($\frac{14}{18}$).

Page 26:

1) (Orange & red) matches (orange & red) ($\frac{1}{2}$), two dark greens ($\frac{2}{4}$), three purples ($\frac{3}{6}$), four greens ($\frac{4}{8}$), six reds ($\frac{6}{12}$) and twelve whites ($\frac{12}{24}$).

2) Brown matches brown ($\frac{1}{3}$), four reds ($\frac{4}{12}$), and eight whites ($\frac{8}{24}$).

3) Dark green matches dark green ($\frac{1}{4}$), two greens ($\frac{2}{8}$), three reds ($\frac{3}{12}$) and six whites ($\frac{6}{24}$).

4) Purple matches purple ($\frac{1}{6}$), two reds ($\frac{2}{12}$), and four whites ($\frac{4}{24}$).

5) (Orange & brown) matches three dark greens ($\frac{3}{4}$), six greens ($\frac{6}{8}$), nine reds ($\frac{9}{12}$) and eighteen whites ($\frac{18}{24}$).

6) Red matches red ($\frac{1}{12}$) and two whites ($\frac{2}{24}$).

7) Yellow matches five whites ($\frac{5}{24}$).

8) Green matches green ($\frac{1}{8}$) and three whites ($\frac{3}{24}$).

9) (Orange & purple) matches seven reds ($\frac{7}{12}$) and fourteen whites ($\frac{14}{24}$).

10) (Orange & yellow) matches five greens ($\frac{5}{8}$) and fifteen whites ($\frac{15}{24}$).

Page 27: 1) purple   2) five whites or yellow   3) four whites or purple   4) six whites or dark green
    three whites or green   three reds or dark green   three reds or dark green   three reds or dark green
     T   T   F   T

Page 28: 1) G (green) 2) R (red) 3) W (white) 4) P (purple) 5) Y (yellow)
6) False, A 7) True, I 8) True, O 9) False, T 10) False, E
11) True, F 12) False, S 13) True, L 14) True, N 15) False, H

T W O   H I P P O S   P L A Y I N G   L E A P   F R O G .
9 3 8   15 7 4 4 8 12   4 13 6 5 7 14 1   13 10 6 4   11 2 8 1

Page 29: 1) G (green) 2) W (white) 3) R (red) 4) P (purple) 5) D (dark green) 6) N (brown)
7) False, T 8) False, E 9) True, I 10) False, U 11) True, O 12) False, C 13) True, B
14) True, L 15) True, H 16) False, S

T H E   B I G G E S T   P O R C U P I N E   I N   T H E   W O R L D .
7 15 8   13 9 1 1 8 16 7   4 11 3 12 10 4 9 6 8   9 6   7 15 8   2 11 3 14 5

Page 30: 1) Y (yellow) 2) R (red) 3) W (white) 4) P (purple)
5) D (dark green) 6) G (green) 7) P (purple) 8) K (black)
9) N (brown) 10) E (blue)
11) False, D 12) False, I 13) True, O 14) True, V
15) False, P 16) True, L 17) False, U 18) True, E
19) True, T 20) False, K

Tillie's   D O   Y O U   L I K E   K I P L I N G ?
Question   5 13   1 13 17   16 12 8 10   8 12 4 16 12 9 6

Millie's   I   D O N ' T   K N O W . I ' V E   N E V E R   K I P P L E D .
Answer   12   5 13 9 19   8 9 13 3   12 14 10   9 10 14 10 2   20 12 15 7 16 18 11

Everything's Coming up Fractions with Cuisenaire Rods   © 1981 Cuisenaire Company of America, Inc.

Page 31:

	Rod color	Family name	Other names
1)	yellow	$\frac{5}{8}$	none
2)	dark green	$\frac{6}{8}$	$\frac{3}{4}$
3)	black	$\frac{7}{8}$	none

Page 32:

1)

Dark green rod family (sixths)

Rod Color	Family name	Other names
red	$\frac{2}{6}$	$\frac{1}{3}$
green	$\frac{3}{6}$	$\frac{1}{2}$
purple	$\frac{4}{6}$	$\frac{2}{3}$
yellow	$\frac{5}{6}$	none

2)

Blue rod family (ninths)

Rod Color	Family name	Other names
red	$\frac{2}{9}$	none
green	$\frac{3}{9}$	$\frac{1}{3}$
black	$\frac{7}{9}$	none
dark green	$\frac{6}{9}$	$\frac{2}{3}$

(Orange & red) rod family (twelfths)

Rod color	Family name	Other names
red	$\frac{2}{12}$	$\frac{1}{6}$
green	$\frac{3}{12}$	$\frac{1}{4}$
purple	$\frac{4}{12}$	$\frac{1}{3}, \frac{2}{6}$
dark green	$\frac{6}{12}$	$\frac{1}{2}, \frac{2}{4}$
brown	$\frac{8}{12}$	$\frac{2}{3}, \frac{4}{6}$
blue	$\frac{9}{12}$	$\frac{3}{4}$
orange	$\frac{10}{12}$	$\frac{5}{6}$

Page 33:

1) $\frac{1}{6} + \frac{2}{3} = \frac{5}{6}$

white + purple = yellow

Place a white and a purple rod end-to-end. Match with yellow to find the sum.

Since yellow = 5 whites and each white = $\frac{1}{6}$, the answer is $\frac{5}{6}$.

2) $\frac{1}{2} + \frac{1}{6} = \frac{4}{6}$ or $\frac{2}{3}$

green + white = 4 whites or 2 reds

Place a green and a white rod end-to-end. Match with purple to find the sum.

There are two possible answers. Purple = 4 whites ($\frac{4}{6}$) or 2 reds ($\frac{2}{3}$). The answer in lowest terms is $\frac{2}{3}$.

54

Page 34: 1) $\frac{1}{2} + \frac{1}{5} = \frac{7}{10}$
yellow + red = black
2) $\frac{1}{5} + \frac{7}{10} = \frac{9}{10}$
red + black = blue
3) $\frac{1}{2} + \frac{3}{10} = \frac{8}{10}$ or $\frac{4}{5}$
yellow + green = 8 whites or 4 reds
4) $\frac{2}{5} + \frac{1}{2} = \frac{9}{10}$
purple + yellow = blue
5) $\frac{1}{10} + \frac{1}{5} = \frac{3}{10}$
white + red = green

6) $\frac{1}{5} + \frac{3}{10} = \frac{5}{10}$ or $\frac{1}{2}$
red + green = 5 whites or yellow
7) $\frac{1}{10} + \frac{3}{5} = \frac{7}{10}$
white + dark green = black
8) $\frac{3}{10} + \frac{1}{10} = \frac{4}{10}$ or $\frac{2}{5}$
green + white = 4 whites or 2 reds
9) $\frac{1}{10} + \frac{5}{10} = \frac{6}{10}$ or $\frac{3}{5}$
white + yellow = 6 whites or 3 reds
10) $\frac{2}{5} + \frac{1}{10} = \frac{5}{10}$ or $\frac{1}{2}$
purple + white = 5 whites or yellow

Page 35: 1) $\frac{1}{2} + \frac{1}{12} = \frac{7}{12}$
dark green + white = black
2) $\frac{1}{4} + \frac{1}{6} = \frac{5}{12}$
green + red = yellow
3) $\frac{1}{6} + \frac{1}{12} = \frac{3}{12}$ or $\frac{1}{4}$
red + white = 3 whites or green
4) $\frac{5}{12} + \frac{1}{6} = \frac{7}{12}$
yellow + red = black
5) $\frac{1}{2} + \frac{1}{6} = \frac{8}{12}$ or $\frac{4}{6}$ or $\frac{2}{3}$
dark green + red = 8 whites or 4 reds or 2 purples

6) $\frac{1}{3} + \frac{1}{12} = \frac{5}{12}$
purple + white = yellow
7) $\frac{1}{4} + \frac{1}{3} = \frac{7}{12}$
green + purple = black
8) $\frac{5}{6} + \frac{1}{12} = \frac{11}{12}$
orange + white = 11 whites
9) $\frac{1}{4} + \frac{1}{12} = \frac{4}{12}$ or $\frac{2}{6}$ or $\frac{1}{3}$
green + white = 4 whites or 2 reds or purple
10) $\frac{2}{3} + \frac{1}{12} = \frac{9}{12}$ or $\frac{3}{4}$
brown + white = 9 whites or 3 greens

Page 36: I.
1) yellow + green = brown $\frac{8}{15}$ T
2) green + white = purple $\frac{4}{15}$ I
3) 2 yellows + white = (orange & white) $\frac{11}{15}$ C
4) 3 greens + yellow = (orange & purple) $\frac{14}{15}$ F

5) yellow + white = dark green $\frac{6}{15}$ N
6) 2 yellows + green = (orange & green) $\frac{13}{15}$ A
7) 2 greens + white = black $\frac{7}{15}$ O
8) 4 whites + 2 greens = orange $\frac{10}{15}$ P

A C O A T O F P A I N T

II.
1) black + red = blue $\frac{9}{14}$ N
2) red + white = green $\frac{3}{14}$ E
3) black + 2 reds = (orange & white) $\frac{11}{14}$ O

4) black + white = brown $\frac{8}{14}$ G
5) 2 reds + white = yellow $\frac{5}{14}$ D
6) black + 3 reds = (orange & green) $\frac{13}{14}$!

D O G G O N E !

Page 37:
1) brown + red = orange $\frac{10}{16}$ U
2) brown + white = blue $\frac{9}{16}$ E
3) purple + white = yellow $\frac{5}{16}$ U
4) brown + 3 reds = (orange & purple) $\frac{14}{16}$ O
5) brown + 5 whites = (orange & green) $\frac{13}{16}$ Y
6) purple + 3 whites = black $\frac{7}{16}$ D

7) brown + purple = (orange & red) = $\frac{12}{16}$ P
8) purple + red = dark green $\frac{6}{16}$ T
9) red + white = green $\frac{3}{16}$ N
10) brown + 3 whites = (orange & white) $\frac{11}{16}$ H
11) 5 reds + 5 whites = (orange & yellow) $\frac{15}{16}$ G
12) white + 7 whites = brown $\frac{8}{16}$ I

T H E Y E N D U P T O N G U E T I E D .

Everything's Coming up Fractions with Cuisenaire Rods   © 1981 Cuisenaire Company of America, Inc.

Page 38:

1) blue + dark green = (orange & yellow) $\frac{15}{18}$ N

2) blue + red = (orange & white) $\frac{11}{18}$ P

3) red + green = yellow $\frac{5}{18}$ E

4) dark green + white = black $\frac{7}{18}$ A

5) green + white = purple $\frac{4}{18}$ S

6) 5 greens + red = (orange & black) $\frac{17}{18}$ H

7) blue + green = (orange & red) $\frac{12}{18}$ R

8) blue + white = orange $\frac{10}{18}$ U

9) dark green + red = brown $\frac{8}{18}$ I

10) green + dark green = blue $\frac{9}{18}$ O

11) red + white = green $\frac{3}{18}$ T

12) blue + 2 reds = (orange & green) $\frac{13}{18}$ D

O N E   S T E P S U P T H E S T A I R S
A N D   T H E   O T H E R   S T A R E S
U P   T H E   S T E P S .

Page 39:

1)

$$\frac{1}{2} = \frac{5}{10}$$
$$+ \frac{2}{5} = \frac{4}{10}$$
$$\frac{9}{10}$$

Check:

$\frac{1}{2}$ of orange = yellow = 5 whites ($\frac{5}{10}$)

$\frac{2}{5}$ of orange = 2 reds = purple = 4 whites ($\frac{4}{10}$)

yellow + purple = blue = 9 whites ($\frac{9}{10}$)

2)

$$\frac{1}{2} = \frac{5}{10}$$
$$+ \frac{1}{10} = \frac{1}{10}$$
$$\frac{6}{10} \text{ or } \frac{3}{5}$$

$\frac{1}{2}$ of orange = yellow = 5 whites ($\frac{5}{10}$)

$\frac{1}{10}$ of orange = white ($\frac{1}{10}$)

yellow + white = dark green = 6 whites ($\frac{6}{10}$)

or 3 reds ($\frac{3}{5}$)

3)

$$\frac{2}{5} = \frac{4}{10}$$
$$+ \frac{1}{10} = \frac{1}{10}$$
$$\frac{5}{10} \text{ or } \frac{1}{2}$$

$\frac{2}{5}$ of orange = 2 reds = purple = 4 whites ($\frac{4}{10}$)

$\frac{1}{10}$ of orange = 1 white ($\frac{1}{10}$)

purple + white = 5 whites ($\frac{5}{10}$)

or yellow ($\frac{1}{2}$)

4)

$$\frac{2}{5} = \frac{4}{10}$$
$$+ \frac{3}{10} = \frac{3}{10}$$
$$\frac{7}{10}$$

$\frac{2}{5}$ of orange = 2 reds = purple = 4 whites ($\frac{4}{10}$)

$\frac{3}{10}$ of orange = green = 3 whites ($\frac{3}{10}$)

purple + green = black = 7 whites ($\frac{7}{10}$)

5)

$$\frac{1}{5} = \frac{2}{10}$$
$$+ \frac{1}{10} = \frac{1}{10}$$
$$\frac{3}{10}$$

$\frac{1}{5}$ of orange = red = 2 whites ($\frac{2}{10}$)

$\frac{1}{10}$ of orange = white ($\frac{1}{10}$)

red + white = green = 3 whites ($\frac{3}{10}$)

6)

$$\frac{1}{2} = \frac{5}{10}$$
$$+ \frac{3}{10} = \frac{3}{10}$$
$$\frac{8}{10} \text{ or } \frac{4}{5}$$

$\frac{1}{2}$ of orange = yellow = 5 whites ($\frac{5}{10}$)

$\frac{3}{10}$ of orange = green = 3 whites ($\frac{3}{10}$)

yellow + green = brown = 8 whites ($\frac{8}{10}$)

or 4 reds ($\frac{4}{5}$)

56

Page 40:

1)
$$\frac{1}{3} = \frac{5}{15}$$
$$+ \frac{1}{5} = \frac{3}{15}$$
R
$$\frac{8}{15}$$

2)
$$\frac{1}{3} = \frac{5}{15}$$
$$+ \frac{2}{5} = \frac{6}{15}$$
K
$$\frac{11}{15}$$

3)
$$\frac{2}{3} = \frac{10}{15}$$
$$+ \frac{1}{5} = \frac{3}{15}$$
A
$$\frac{13}{15}$$

4)
$$\frac{3}{5} = \frac{9}{15}$$
$$+ \frac{1}{3} = \frac{5}{15}$$
I
$$\frac{14}{15}$$

5)
$$\frac{1}{3} = \frac{5}{15}$$
$$+ \frac{1}{15} = \frac{1}{15}$$
L
$$\frac{6}{15} \text{ or } \frac{2}{5}$$

6)
$$\frac{1}{5} = \frac{3}{15}$$
$$+ \frac{7}{15} = \frac{7}{15}$$
C
$$\frac{10}{15} \text{ or } \frac{2}{3}$$

7)
$$\frac{4}{15} = \frac{4}{15}$$
$$+ \frac{1}{3} = \frac{5}{15}$$
T
$$\frac{9}{15} \text{ or } \frac{3}{5}$$

8)
$$\frac{2}{5} = \frac{6}{15}$$
$$+ \frac{1}{15} = \frac{1}{15}$$
U
$$\frac{7}{15}$$

9)
$$\frac{2}{3} = \frac{10}{15}$$
$$+ \frac{2}{15} = \frac{2}{15}$$
M
$$\frac{12}{15} \text{ or } \frac{4}{5}$$

Riddle
Answer   A M I L K   T R U C K

Page 41:

1)
$$\frac{7}{12} = \frac{7}{12}$$
$$+ \frac{5}{6} = \frac{10}{12}$$
$$\frac{17}{12}$$
$$\text{or } 1\frac{5}{12}$$

2)
$$\frac{3}{4} = \frac{9}{12}$$
$$+ \frac{2}{3} = \frac{8}{12}$$
$$\frac{17}{12}$$
$$\text{or } 1\frac{5}{12}$$

3)
$$\frac{5}{12} = \frac{5}{12}$$
$$+ \frac{2}{3} = \frac{8}{12}$$
$$\frac{13}{12}$$
$$\text{or } 1\frac{1}{12}$$

4)
$$\frac{5}{6} = \frac{10}{12}$$
$$+ \frac{3}{4} = \frac{9}{12}$$
$$\frac{19}{12}$$
$$\text{or } 1\frac{7}{12}$$

Page 42:

1) $\frac{5}{8} - \frac{1}{4} = \frac{3}{8}$
yellow – red = green

2) $\frac{7}{8} - \frac{1}{2} = \frac{3}{8}$
black – purple = green

3) $\frac{7}{8} - \frac{3}{4} = \frac{1}{8}$
black – dark green = white

Place a yellow and a red rod side-by-side. The difference is green.
   green = 3 whites ($\frac{3}{8}$)
Place a black and a purple rod side-by-side. The difference is green.
   green = 3 whites ($\frac{3}{8}$)
Place a black and a dark green rod side-by-side. The difference is white ($\frac{1}{8}$).

Page 43:

1) $\frac{1}{2} - \frac{1}{3} = \frac{1}{6}$
green – red = white

2) $\frac{1}{3} - \frac{1}{6} = \frac{1}{6}$
red – white = white

3) $\frac{2}{3} - \frac{1}{2} = \frac{1}{6}$
purple – green = white

4) $\frac{2}{3} - \frac{1}{6} = \frac{3}{6}$ or $\frac{1}{2}$
purple – white = 3 whites or green

5) $\frac{5}{6} - \frac{1}{3} = \frac{3}{6}$ or $\frac{1}{2}$
yellow – red = 3 whites or green

6) $\frac{1}{2} - \frac{1}{6} = \frac{2}{6}$ or $\frac{1}{3}$
green – white = 2 whites or red

7) $\frac{5}{6} - \frac{1}{2} = \frac{2}{6}$ or $\frac{1}{3}$
yellow – green = 2 whites or red

8) $\frac{5}{6} - \frac{2}{3} = \frac{1}{6}$
yellow – purple = white

57

Everything's Coming up Fractions with Cuisenaire Rods   © 1981 Cuisenaire Company of America, Inc.

Page 44:

1) $\frac{1}{2} - \frac{1}{4} = \frac{2}{8}$ or $\frac{1}{4}$
purple − red = 2 whites or red

2) $\frac{1}{2} - \frac{1}{8} = \frac{3}{8}$
purple − white = green

3) $\frac{3}{4} - \frac{1}{2} = \frac{2}{8}$ or $\frac{1}{4}$
dark green − purple = 2 whites or red

4) $\frac{3}{4} - \frac{1}{8} = \frac{5}{8}$
dark green − white = yellow

5) $\frac{3}{8} - \frac{1}{4} = \frac{1}{8}$
green − red = white

6) $\frac{5}{8} - \frac{1}{2} = \frac{1}{8}$
yellow − purple = white

7) $\frac{7}{8} - \frac{1}{4} = \frac{5}{8}$
black − red = yellow

8) $\frac{7}{8} - \frac{3}{4} = \frac{1}{8}$
black − dark green = white

9) $\frac{5}{8} - \frac{1}{4} = \frac{3}{8}$
yellow − red = green

10) $\frac{3}{4} - \frac{5}{8} = \frac{1}{8}$
dark green − yellow = white

11) $1 - \frac{1}{4} = \frac{6}{8}$ or $\frac{3}{4}$
brown − red = 6 whites or 3 red

12) $1 - \frac{3}{8} = \frac{5}{8}$
brown − green = yellow

Page 45:

1) blue − red = black $\frac{7}{18}$ Y

2) blue − white = brown $\frac{8}{18}$ A

3) dark green − red = purple $\frac{4}{18}$ T

4) dark green − white = yellow $\frac{5}{18}$ O

5) green − red = white $\frac{1}{18}$ N

6) 2 dark greens − red = orange $\frac{10}{18}$ M

7) 2 dark greens − white = (orange & white) $\frac{11}{18}$ B

8) 5 greens − red = (orange & green) $\frac{13}{18}$ S

9) 5 greens − white = (orange & purple) $\frac{14}{18}$ I

10) 8 reds − 1 white = (orange & yellow) $\frac{15}{18}$ U

11) 7 reds − 2 dark greens = red $\frac{2}{18}$ H

12) 4 reds − 5 whites = green $\frac{3}{18}$ E

13) blue − green = dark green $\frac{6}{18}$ R

14) (orange & brown) − white = (orange & black) $\frac{17}{18}$ D

O N E   I S   A   M A D   B U N N Y   A N D
T H E   O T H E R   I S   B A D   M O N E Y

Page 46:

1)

$\frac{1}{6} = \frac{2}{12}$
$- \frac{1}{12} = \frac{1}{12}$
$\frac{1}{12}$

Check:
$\frac{1}{6}$ of (orange & red) = red = 2 whites ($\frac{2}{12}$)
$\frac{1}{12}$ of (orange & red) = white ($\frac{1}{12}$)
red − white = white ($\frac{1}{12}$)

2)

$\frac{1}{4} = \frac{3}{12}$
$- \frac{1}{6} = \frac{2}{12}$
$\frac{1}{12}$

$\frac{1}{4}$ of (orange & red) = green = 3 whites ($\frac{3}{12}$)
$\frac{1}{6}$ of (orange & red) = 2 whites ($\frac{2}{12}$)
green − red = white ($\frac{1}{12}$)

3)

$\frac{3}{4} = \frac{9}{12}$
$- \frac{1}{3} = \frac{4}{12}$
$\frac{5}{12}$

$\frac{3}{4}$ of (orange & red) = 3 greens = blue = 9 whites ($\frac{9}{12}$)
$\frac{1}{3}$ of (orange & red) = purple = 4 whites ($\frac{4}{12}$)
blue − purple = yellow ($\frac{5}{12}$)

4)

$\frac{5}{6} = \frac{10}{12}$
$- \frac{1}{4} = \frac{3}{12}$
$\frac{7}{12}$

$\frac{5}{6}$ of (orange & red) = 5 reds = orange = 10 whites ($\frac{10}{12}$)
$\frac{1}{4}$ of (orange & red) = green = 3 whites ($\frac{3}{12}$)
orange − green = black ($\frac{7}{12}$)

5)

$\frac{5}{6} = \frac{10}{12}$
$- \frac{7}{12} = \frac{7}{12}$
$\frac{3}{12}$ or $\frac{1}{4}$

$\frac{5}{6}$ of (orange & red) = 5 reds = orange = 10 whites ($\frac{10}{12}$)
$\frac{7}{12}$ of (orange & red) = black = 7 whites ($\frac{7}{12}$)
orange − black = 3 whites ($\frac{3}{12}$)
or green ($\frac{1}{4}$)

6)

$\frac{3}{4} = \frac{9}{12}$
$- \frac{5}{12} = \frac{5}{12}$
$\frac{4}{12}$ or $\frac{1}{3}$

$\frac{3}{4}$ of (orange & red) = 3 greens = blue = 9 whites ($\frac{9}{12}$)
$\frac{5}{12}$ of (orange & red) = yellow = 5 whites ($\frac{5}{12}$)
blue − yellow = 4 whites ($\frac{4}{12}$)
or purple ($\frac{1}{3}$)

58

Page 47:

1)
$$\frac{5}{16} = \frac{5}{16}$$
$$-\frac{1}{4} = \frac{4}{16}$$
$$\frac{1}{16}$$

2)
$$\frac{5}{8} = \frac{10}{16}$$
$$-\frac{3}{16} = \frac{3}{16}$$
$$\frac{7}{16}$$

3)
$$\frac{3}{4} = \frac{12}{16}$$
$$-\frac{1}{16} = \frac{1}{16}$$
$$\frac{11}{16}$$

4)
$$\frac{1}{2} = \frac{8}{16}$$
$$-\frac{3}{16} = \frac{3}{16}$$
$$\frac{5}{16}$$

5)
$$\frac{7}{8} = \frac{14}{16}$$
$$-\frac{5}{16} = \frac{5}{16}$$
$$\frac{9}{16}$$

6)
$$\frac{9}{16} = \frac{9}{16}$$
$$-\frac{3}{8} = \frac{6}{16}$$
$$\frac{3}{16}$$

7)
$$\frac{15}{16} = \frac{15}{16}$$
$$-\frac{1}{2} = \frac{8}{16}$$
$$\frac{7}{16}$$

8)
$$\frac{3}{4} = \frac{12}{16}$$
$$-\frac{7}{16} = \frac{7}{16}$$
$$\frac{5}{16}$$

9)
$$\frac{15}{16} = \frac{15}{16}$$
$$-\frac{1}{8} = \frac{2}{16}$$
$$\frac{13}{16}$$

Page 48:

1)
$$\frac{5}{12} = \frac{5}{12}$$
$$+\frac{1}{4} = \frac{3}{12}$$
$$\frac{8}{12} \text{ or } \frac{2}{3} \quad D$$

2)
$$\frac{1}{4} = \frac{3}{12}$$
$$-\frac{1}{6} = \frac{2}{12}$$
$$\frac{1}{12} \quad I$$

3)
$$\frac{1}{4} = \frac{3}{12}$$
$$+\frac{1}{6} = \frac{2}{12}$$
$$\frac{5}{12} \quad T$$

4)
$$\frac{5}{6} = \frac{10}{12}$$
$$-\frac{1}{4} = \frac{3}{12}$$
$$\frac{7}{12} \quad C$$

5)
$$\frac{2}{3} = \frac{8}{12}$$
$$+\frac{1}{4} = \frac{3}{12}$$
$$\frac{11}{12} \quad Y$$

6)
$$\frac{5}{12} = \frac{5}{12}$$
$$-\frac{1}{4} = \frac{3}{12}$$
$$\frac{2}{12} \text{ or } \frac{1}{6} \quad K$$

7)
$$\frac{1}{12} = \frac{1}{12}$$
$$+\frac{1}{6} = \frac{2}{12}$$
$$\frac{3}{12} \text{ or } \frac{1}{4} \quad S$$

8)
$$\frac{5}{6} = \frac{10}{12}$$
$$-\frac{1}{2} = \frac{6}{12}$$
$$\frac{4}{12} \text{ or } \frac{1}{3} \quad R$$

9)
$$\frac{2}{3} = \frac{8}{12}$$
$$+\frac{1}{12} = \frac{1}{12}$$
$$\frac{9}{12} \text{ or } \frac{3}{4} \quad A$$

Riddle
Answer

A	Y	A	R	D	S	T	I	C	K
$\frac{3}{4}$	$\frac{11}{12}$	$\frac{3}{4}$	$\frac{1}{3}$	$\frac{2}{3}$	$\frac{1}{4}$	$\frac{5}{12}$	$\frac{1}{12}$	$\frac{7}{12}$	$\frac{1}{6}$.

Page 49:

1)
$$\frac{1}{2} = \frac{9}{18}$$
$$+\frac{5}{18} = \frac{5}{18}$$
$$\frac{14}{18} \text{ or } \frac{7}{9} \quad G$$

2)
$$\frac{1}{2} = \frac{9}{18}$$
$$+\frac{4}{9} = \frac{8}{18}$$
$$\frac{17}{18} \quad P$$

3)
$$\frac{5}{6} = \frac{15}{18}$$
$$+\frac{1}{18} = \frac{1}{18}$$
$$\frac{16}{18} \text{ or } \frac{8}{9} \quad T$$

4)
$$\frac{4}{9} = \frac{8}{18}$$
$$+\frac{1}{6} = \frac{3}{18}$$
$$\frac{11}{18} \quad N$$

5)
$$\frac{2}{9} = \frac{4}{18}$$
$$+\frac{5}{18} = \frac{5}{18}$$
$$\frac{9}{18} = \frac{1}{2} \quad E$$

6)
$$\frac{1}{6} = \frac{3}{18}$$
$$+\frac{7}{18} = \frac{7}{18}$$
$$\frac{10}{18} = \frac{5}{9} \quad R$$

7)
$$\frac{8}{9} = \frac{16}{18}$$
$$-\frac{1}{2} = \frac{9}{18}$$
$$\frac{7}{18} \quad H$$

8)
$$\frac{5}{6} = \frac{15}{18}$$
$$-\frac{2}{3} = \frac{12}{18}$$
$$\frac{3}{18} = \frac{1}{6} \quad I$$

9)
$$\frac{1}{2} = \frac{9}{18}$$
$$-\frac{4}{9} = \frac{8}{18}$$
$$\frac{1}{18} \quad S$$

10)
$$\frac{2}{3} = \frac{12}{18}$$
$$-\frac{7}{18} = \frac{7}{18}$$
$$\frac{5}{18} \quad U$$

11)
$$\frac{5}{6} = \frac{15}{18}$$
$$-\frac{1}{9} = \frac{2}{18}$$
$$\frac{13}{18} \quad L$$

12)
$$\frac{11}{18} = \frac{11}{18}$$
$$-\frac{1}{2} = \frac{9}{18}$$
$$\frac{2}{18} \text{ or } \frac{1}{9} \quad O$$

H	E	G	E	T	S	S	P	L	I	N	T	E	R	S	I	N	H	I	S	T	O	N	G	U	E
$\frac{7}{18}$	$\frac{1}{2}$	$\frac{7}{9}$	$\frac{1}{2}$	$\frac{8}{9}$	$\frac{1}{18}$	$\frac{1}{18}$	$\frac{17}{18}$	$\frac{13}{18}$	$\frac{1}{6}$	$\frac{11}{18}$	$\frac{8}{9}$	$\frac{1}{2}$	$\frac{5}{9}$	$\frac{1}{18}$	$\frac{1}{6}$	$\frac{11}{18}$	$\frac{7}{18}$	$\frac{1}{6}$	$\frac{1}{18}$	$\frac{8}{9}$	$\frac{1}{9}$	$\frac{11}{18}$	$\frac{7}{9}$	$\frac{5}{18}$	$\frac{1}{2}$.

NO LONGER THE PROPERTY OF THE UNIVERSITY OF R. I. LIBRARY

Everything's Coming up Fractions with Cuisenaire Rods   © 1981 Cuisenaire Company of America, Inc.